It's a long way to MALTA

An Irishman's 'Gem in the Med'

PADDY CUMMINS

First published in 2012 by Bridge Publishing

All characters in this publications are fictitious, and any resemblance to real persons, living or dead, is purely coincidental.

ISBN
978-953-8419-54-6

Printed at
Blackdot Printers, Malta - Europe
admin@blackdotprinters.com

Bridge Publishing
Campile. Co. Wexford.

To all my cherished friends in Malta.

Introduction

When the name on your passport is Patrick, and the name on your back is Paddy, the whole world knows you're an Irishman. Sometimes I think I'd like to hide the fact, but the old brogue gives me away. I have considered a bit of tweaking, but I think it's too late now. With my name firmly etched on the covers of ten books, I am surely irreversibly branded for life.

In Ireland, I certainly wouldn't have many hiding places. After a lifetime of throwing my hat into a myriad of rings: a showband stint, a political foray, a horseracing odyssey, various business adventures, a forty-year marriage, and a large clutch of disparate youngsters, I am surely now well and truly documented.

Perhaps that's why Malta agreed with me so well when by mere chance I wandered there ten years ago and have regarded it as my 'home from home' ever since. Now, I have to admit that I'm a bit of a loner – it may have come from early shyness, or a touch of inferiority complex, I'm not sure. You see, I can be happy, contented, and at ease in my own company for long periods. Of course I have nothing against good company, especially with a little drop of something to banish the inhibitions, but I have to say that I do enjoy observing people, and I prefer to be in the shadows, inconspicuous on the fringes of conversation, than to be in the thick of it. For all those years I managed to get away with that in Malta, and I must say it's a great place for observation and eavesdropping, but now I'm not so sure; I think I may have blown my cover. That Maltese book I wrote on an extended visit in 2008, and now in all the bookshops on the island, has probably ensured that my preference for privacy will hardly be respected on this visit, but sure what can I do? I can't have my cake and eat it.'

****

It's a long way to Malta

"This is your Captain speaking...we are about to start our descent, and should be landing at Luqa Airport in approximately fifteen minutes...the weather in Malta is fine with bright sunshine and temperatures of twenty-one degrees in a light breeze...thank you for flying with Ryanair and we wish you a pleasant stay in Malta."

Excellent! That's pure music to my ears. Twenty-one degrees! Some change from the frost and ice we left behind in Dublin this morning. I put the watch forward an hour, fold up the sleeves of the shirt to expose the white arms, and slide the little window shutter up, to get a view of Gozo as we glide in.

This has been a dream flight, not even one *'fasten your seatbelt'* request and hardly a tremble of turbulence - I'm always wary of the Alps reacting menacingly to our invasion of their airspace – and for a petrified flyer like me, a smooth flight is a heavenly relief. On my last visit I was sure we would hit Malta with a bang. The pilot calmly addressed us as we approached – I'm always in awe of their ability to convey an air of normality and we only seconds away from an impending disaster – *"We will shortly be landing at Luqa Airport...but first we have to descend through some nasty little thunder*

clouds…there will be some slight turbulence…but we should land on time."
Slight turbulence!!! It was like tumbling down concrete steps; I was terror-stricken. But 'all's well that ends well,' and despite my visions of death, we brushed the tarmac gently in the correct spot and taxied towards the terminal to a fanfare of: *"Ryanair…the low fares airline that always gets you there on time."*

I remember back to my first visit. God, it doesn't seem like ten years ago at all – but it is. Approaching from the air, the little tapestry of landscape that is the Maltese Islands looked a bit arid and austere; I wasn't impressed. I don't really know what I was expecting – something grander, I suppose, more imposing; I'm not sure. Anyway, having explored and enjoyed almost every square mile of it since then, I have come to love, not only the landscape, but the history and culture, the friendly, warm-hearted people, and a host of other attributes that make this a special little place for me.

Having gorged myself with deep breaths of clear, warm Maltese air as I stepped off the plane and passed through the terminal, I'm now relaxing with a cappuccino and 'The Times of Malta,' as I await my favourite taxi. Charlie De Marco has been driving me now for about five years. I ring him when I land – "Paddy The Irishman has arrived," and although he is based about ten miles away, his big black Mercedes would speed into the airport before I'd finished my coffee, and whisk me off to Salina Bay in a welter of wit, news and banter.

Charlie is an interesting character and a good example of the bright young Maltese go-getters who are willing to work hard and strive for every opportunity to enhance their quality of life and the future of their country. Although still in his twenties, he has a small garage business, a lucrative taxi service, and is a member of the local council, representing the Labour Party.
He arrives with his trade mark broad smile. We're away.
I ask Charlie about his current love life. The last time we talked, he hinted at something exciting he was exploring. Another broad smile lights up his big bronze face, and his hands play on the steering wheel. There's a happy glint in his eye.
"C'mon, you can tell me; t'will be safe with the Irishman."
He laughs, hesitates, and then spits it out.
"You won't believe this."
"Try me."
"My new girlfriend is the Mayor of the council…"
"The Mayor! Well done…great stuff…that should work…two politicians…"
"Yes…should work…should work…one big problem…"
"What's the problem, Charlie? Sure it's a match 'made in heaven'…"
"She is The Nationalist Party, and me, The Labour Party"
Oh! The penny drops. I'm now fairly well versed in the politics of Malta. I know all about the intense and sometimes bitter rivalry between the two main parties on the island. Only one seat divides them in parliament and they are constantly at war.
"And there's more." Charlie isn't finished yet. "Her father is a minister in the government."

"Well Charlie, all I can do is wish you luck; if this works out for you, as they say in Ireland: *'You'll never see a poor day again.'*"

Charlie is a fast driver and the airport road is now very good. We are soon speeding along the new road that EU money helped to create to the delight of those crazy young Maltese speedsters - 'Formula 1' drivers who make up their own rules of the road as they rocket by.
We whiz by the towering edifice of Mdina, 'The Silent City.'
"Slow down, Charlie."
"Why; you scared?"
"No, just want to get a good look at things; what's the hurry?"
He eases his foot, looks across at me with a disbelieving frown.
"How long you come to Malta?"
"Ten years."
"So, the same everything is still."
I sometimes have to smile at the sequence of words the Maltese use in an English sentence.
"I know, Charlie, but Mdina; that always seems to stir something in me. I don't know what it is about it, but when I go in there and wander around the little narrow streets, I get an eerie feeling of strange spiritualism, like I was trespassing in an old ghost town. Maybe it's just me, or am I imagining things?"
"No, the same lots of people feel; because it *is* an old ghost town; you know, The Silent City."
We pass through Ta' Qali. I have walked around this area several times. This used to be the headquarters of the

Airforce during World War Two, the scene of courage and heroism, as young pilots patrolled the skies and kept Malta from the evil clutches of the enemy. Now on the site, occupying the old army huts, is a 'Craft Village.' The huts are barely held together with rust, but it doesn't stop tourists flocking there to buy the unique Maltese hand-made crafts.

Charlie shows me the new National Conference Centre.

"All the big things are held there now."

"You mean conferences, shows, exhibitions?"

"Yes, big concerts too. Tom Jones was here."

"Did you go?"

"No, too busy working."

"You're a workaholic, Charlie."

We pass the Aviation Museum.

"You ever in there?" Charlie asks, as he slows to a crawl.

"Yeah, a couple of times. Fascinating to see all the old warplanes: Spitfires, Hurricanes, Gladiators and all the other old Airforce stuff."

Charlie tells me that they recently raised another old Gladiator from the floor of the sea, and it's now being restored.

"I'm all for that, Charlie. The heroic deeds of those brave young pilots deserves to be documented and remembered."

"Many of them are in there," says Charlie, as we pass the Military Cemetery, just outside Ta' Qali.

"I know, I've spent many hours in there wandering through the rows of graves. All young lads in their teens and twenties; what a waste of young lives."

"Yes," says Charlie, "but they had to die to save Malta."

Before we accelerate out of Ta Qali, I take the opportunity to get a little rise on my taxi driver. We are passing The National Stadium, with its big impressive entrance.

"Any big international matches there recently?"

A loaded question for sure, because I had read in the Malta Times that Malta had been well beaten by Georgia in a 'Friendly' only a couple of weeks ago.

"Not any games recently, the last one was a while ago."

For a football fanatic like Charlie, that answer was as vague and evasive as I expected.

"What about the game two weeks ago when Malta were hammered by that little team from Georgia?"

"I prefer not to speak about it," he replies with embarrassment written all over his face.

"Okay, okay, we'll both forget it then."

A quick glance across, a little smile, a pause, then: "Thank you."

We travel the last mile in silence, arriving safely at the glass-fronted, elegant façade of 'The Wavecrest Hotel'.

****

Check in

When the Macallef Brothers decided in 1980 to build a new hotel, and began looking around for a suitable site in the Salina Bay area – the sunniest corner of Malta – they got lucky. The rocky shoreline surrounding the bay had just been earmarked for major development. A new road skirting the sea all the way to St. Paul's Bay was the main feature of the plan, but of course that was the key that unlocked this prime location for the provision of hotels, apartments, private dwellings and shops. The brothers were in the right place at the right time.

It was by no means easy. The rocks sloped far inland from the seabed in a mass of uneven terrain, the road would sit on a levelled shelf, and any hotel requiring access to the sea would have to design and build cleverly underneath the new road. This was no bother to the Macallef Brothers. Not only did they construct a fine eight-story, four-hundred-bed hotel, but they succeeded in locating the massive dining room and ballroom directly underneath the road. Their ingenuity didn't stop there. This wide access beneath the road enabled them to utilise the sea frontage for a luxury pool, and a sunbathing area that has since been sending bronze bodies back home to all corners of the globe.

I discovered 'The Wavecrest Hotel' during my first visit to Malta, and have been part of the furniture there ever since. A complete stranger to the island and not a very discerning traveller, I took the easy road and left everything to my friendly travel agent. The hotel they put me in was grand, comfortable, good food, lovely staff and guests, and I would have been perfectly happy to return there on my next visit. But, as it frequently does, 'Fate' intervened. I went for a seaside walk one lovely sunny Maltese day. Down to St. Paul's Bay, up the new road, hugging the water, through Bugibba and around Salina Bay. Suddenly I found myself in a different Malta. The sea was a blue I hadn't seen before, the sun seemed more soothing and caressing than any sun I had known, and the feeling of wellbeing and contentment I felt at that spot, I can feel to this day. The 'Wavecrest' dominated, and of course, 'Fate' directed my steps into the reception desk. The rest, as they say, is history.

I follow Charlie through the big revolving glass door into the wide expanse of the impressive foyer. He drops my case at the reception desk, I pay him, he gives me a warm Maltese 'thank you' handshake, and exits the hotel.

I feel lucky. Though I can't see him, I recognise the voice of my favourite receptionist, Alberto, coming from the office behind the desk. With a sweeping look around the foyer I see lots of movement, people leisurely strolling towards the restaurant, casually perusing the shopping mall or meandering around the games and 'Internet' areas. Unusually, I am the only one checking in. Alberto suddenly appears, his eyes focused on a ledger, into

which he makes an entry, before resuming a phone conversation in Maltese that seemed to have been stalled temporarily. Free again, he turns his gaze in my direction, recognises me, and with a big, wide-eyed, welcoming smile, shakes my hand vigorously, chanting:
"You're welcome, Mr Cummins, you're welcome!"
A great start for me.
Like the cruel Irish sod that I am, I immediately put Alberto's welcome and affection for me to the test.
"Now Alberto, I know you are glad to see me, but what have you got for me?"
"Oh yes, the room; let me check; how long are you staying?"
"Four weeks."
He opens the desktop window.
"Yes, I see; you have booked from 7th January to 7th February. Thirty-one days, long stay rates and no single supplement. Your room is number 341 on the third floor."
"Great, thank you, Alberto - a 'sea view' room, as usual?"
"No, Mr Cummins, I'm sorry; it's overlooking the courtyard."
"Alberto, I thought you said I was welcome."
"Yes, of course you are welcome, my friend."
"Well, giving me that room doesn't make me feel very welcome. That room is in 'knickersland.' All I'd have there is a bird's eye view of the sky and an exhibition of lady's underwear hanging from every balcony. You know I always stay in a 'sea view' room"
"But those rooms are a special rate, Mr Cummins."

"And I am a special guest, Alberto. Ten years, ten years, I'm coming here, is that loyalty? C'mon now, Alberto, get on that computer and find me a decent room."

On my first stay at the hotel I was given a 'courtyard' room. I wasn't yet wise to the huge advantage of a 'sea view' room, but on the advice of a friendly guest at breakfast one morning, I paid extra, upgraded, and have been feasting on the blue Med from my balcony ever since. To-day, I just feel that after all my loyalty over the years, I deserve the concession of a 'sea view' room at no extra charge, and I'm determined to cajole Alberto to oblige.

He checks the computer screen.

"Number 814 on the eight floor is available. I'll tell you the extra charge."

"Don't bother, Alberto, Just book me in to it and forget about the extra."

"My job will be gone because of crazy Irishman."

He played the keyboard.

"Thank you, Alberto, if you lose your job, you can come and work in Ireland."

He handed me the key to 814, a room looking out over the blue Mediterranean, and with the best view in Malta.

****

Pub Crawl

As everyone knows, Irishmen like a drink – well, perhaps *drinks* would be a more accurate way of putting it – and I have to admit I'm no exception to that rule. For more years than I care to remember, I have subscribed to Benjemin Franklin's view that: *"Beer is proof that God loves us and wants us to be happy,"* and I also swear to the old Irish proverb that: *"What whiskey will not cure, there is no cure for."*

Why wouldn't I? Sure wasn't I reared on it. How the Irish perfected the art of drinking has exercised the minds of clever people world-wide. It's a mysterious phenomenon, and almost akin to any of 'the great wonders of the world.' If only they had bothered to ask me, I would have explained.

You see, drinking in Ireland is the most important element of our culture, and treating the pub as a second home has been a way of life since God was a boy. When the Irish are in the pub, you can be sure of one thing; they are drinking, and I mean *real drinking* – not like the English or the Americans, who use the pint to adorn the little table in front of them, and to occasionally wet their lips with it. But drinking isn't the only thing that brings the Irish to the pub. It's the togetherness thing, the gossip, the banter, the sessions, and of course, the antics and the utterances of so many 'larger than life' characters, that turns this social exercise into a heavenly ecstasy, banishing their inhibitions and enriching their spirits.

You see then, that the Irish only drink to give them a little escape from reality, and they firmly believe in the old saying: *"Reality is an illusion that occurs due to the lack of alcohol."*

When I first landed in Malta, one of my first priorities was to search for an Irish pub. I enquired and was directed to several. I found 'Murphy's,' 'O'Connor's,' 'Molly Malone's,' 'The Dubliner' 'O'Reilly's' and a few others. They were all over the island, but I have to tell you, except for one, near St. Paul's Bay, I failed to find another real Irish pub. You see, they didn't have the one basic requirement: an Irish governor or an Irish landlady. I mean – just look at it like this - an Irish pub with Maltese owners and staff – gimme a break. To pick an old Irish name and hang it in the middle of shamrocks and leprechauns on the outside of a bar, on the pretence that it is Irish is a trick, that for me, doesn't work.

The one near St. Paul's Bay is the genuine article, and I always enjoy it – pity it's a bit out of my way – too far to stagger home. But all was not lost. I found the next best thing – a little English pub that had character, atmosphere, friendliness and charm - the nearest in Malta to an Irish pub, and only around the corner from my hotel.

***

Having savoured the beauty of an orange sun descending over a calm blue sea, I retreat from my sun-drenched balcony to the coolness of my bedroom. I decide to leave the unpacking 'till to-morrow - it was a long day and I'm not really up to it. I'm feeling a bit weary or maybe it's just laziness. But I could *'down'* a good drop of Maltese liquor, and a couple of pints of 'Cisk'. I think I could handle that alright. Not a bad idea at all. With a new spurt of energy, I quickly throw a shape on myself, exit the hotel, and head for Roy's Bar'.
Now, I have to tell you, Roy's pub is a little gem. Perched on the corner of a high block of apartments and elevated a few feet above street level, the location is perfect, and the drinkers, mostly British, sit leisurely around tables on the outside veranda, enjoying their beer, their smokes, and their life, oblivious to the passing traffic, and the problems of the big wide world.

I climb the steps and enter. The bar is long, narrow, with a short counter, which is laden with ten large taps for various draught beers. A few high stools flank the counter and are fully occupied, likewise the tables and chairs that stretch down by one wall to the far end, where the two little toilets are squeezed together.

Roy is busy serving a table, but sharp as ever, he cops me in the corner of one eye. His appearance never changes – still has the dark tee-shirt, jeans and platform shoes, the tight beard that circles his small mouth from nose to chin,

the shiny bald head, and the friendly half-smile that never leaves his face. Small and slightly plump, he has a high-pitched voice, especially when laughing or excitable, and he is now almost falsetto as he exclaims:
"Oh Jasus, the Irishman is back!"
After a vigorous handshake and a bear hug, he calms down, and in his typical courteous British manner asks:
"What would you like?"
"I'll try a 'house double' scotch."
"Ice and lemonade?"
"Aye, sure I might as well."
"When did you arrive?"
"About an hour ago."
"How long this time?"
"Oh, I don't know – four weeks, I hope – until I get bored or broke – I'll have to play it by ear."

Roy is his usual bubbly self, bristling with charm and good humour, chatting to everyone, running a full bar on his own with clockwork efficiency. Most of his clientele are retired British couples on long-stay winter holidays. Some are living in nearby apartments, having relocated to Malta on retirement. They come for the excellent climate, the attractive winter accommodation packages, the low cost of living, and the welcoming, friendly Maltese. Roy's bar seems to draw them like a magnet – it's like a home from home for them – and sometimes I get the feeling that it's a 'Day Care Centre' for senior citizens of England, Scotland and Wales.

I find a seat between two tables. This allows me the choice to rest my glass on either table, but more importantly, the luxury to overhear the issues being debated at either side of me. In no time I have the names of the four on my left and the three on my right.

Len and Gloria are endeavouring to convince Ron and Judy of the severity of Len's arthritis. It's serious stuff. Len gives an example.

"Do you know, Ron, I can't get in or out of the bath, and if I shower I can't bend down to wash my lower body!!"

He appears to be in his mid-eighties, and, apart from a little stiffness, seems to be in fairly good shape. His wife looks a good bit younger, but somewhat heavier. Ron turns to Gloria.

"Now Gloria, it's over to you. That's where you come in handy – a labour of love."

She looks unimpressed - I would say even a bit alarmed at the suggestion.

"Oh, I couldn't do that."

"Why not?" Ron seems intent on winding her up. "A little bit of scrubbing down stairs – make a new man of him."

Judy joins in the fun. "Might make a new woman of you too, Gloria."

Len looks a bit embarrassed, and perhaps sorry for raising the issue at all. It ends in laughter, and the suggestion from Ron that as a last resort he should try getting a sponge on a long handle, and with directions from above, to navigate around the crevices below.

The ones on my right are an elderly couple chatting to a well-groomed gentleman with a swanky walking stick. Steve and Jenny are from Liverpool and Frank is from Devon. Now I have to admit that not all retired British men are overweight, but the ones I meet in Roy's bar certainly have one thing in common – they are barrel-types with enormous potbellies. It must be the drink or perhaps it's the big meals and the leisurely lifestyles, or more likely, a combination of all three. Whatever the reason, I have to say one thing about big obese men in a pub – they are invariably friendly, relaxed, and as they say in Ireland: *Happy as Larry.*

Steve is certainly one of these. He is sprawled over the chair, his chubby fingers clasped around his giant stomach, and a big broad smile illuminating his flushed, full-moon face. Jenny is slim and prim, and as a couple, they seem to radiate happiness and affection. Frank is a tall, handsome, elegant man, around the eighty mark. He speaks with a cultured, neutral accent, and I'm certain he has travelled the world.

The conversation is polite and in general terms, with no contentious issues raised – my left ear has by far the better entertainment. Steve hoists himself upright and carefully swivels his belly in the direction of the toilet. On returning, he seems to be a bit agitated – the big smile is replaced by a look of annoyance. He flops down on the chair, beckons to Roy who is passing by.
"What did you do to the loo?"
Roy smiles broadly.
"Had a new sliding door fitted yesterday – like it?"
"Like it! It's a bloody disaster!"
"Why, Steve? Double doors – more privacy."
"It's too bloody small for two doors – a man can't sit down and have a proper pee."

He lifts himself up again, stretches his bright green tee-shirt out in front.
"Look, I pissed on my new tee-shirt!"
On close inspection by most of the bar's drinkers, the truth of Steve's statement is there for all to see. Roy is speechless momentarily, but hasn't time to discuss the matter further.
"Sorry, Steve old boy."
"Sorry won't fix my new shirt."
"Oh, alright then, I'll buy you a bloody shirt!" His voice raises an octave. *"But the fucking door stays – cost me a fucking fortune!"*
Steve recovers his composure and replaces the lost liquid with a good helping from his pint, oblivious to the enjoyment his fellow-drinkers are deriving from his little mishap.

Roy emerges again loaded with bowls of snack biscuits – one for every table. Now, while I always appreciate these little gestures, and, in fairness, many pubs in Malta make them, I try to stick to the drink. Not that I have anything against the treats, but, as you well know, they are full of calories, and in my case, the drink puts more than enough weight on me, without adding more with snacks.

But of course, after a few beers you lose your sense of reason and your resolve to mind the figure. I begin with one, return for two and soon I'm nibbling away to my heart's content, proving once again the truth of Oscar Wilde's contention: "*We can resist everything except temptation.*" Soon I'm savouring the salt-laden titbits, a thirst-inducing trick of Roy's, designed to enhance his sales and inflate his coffers. But nobody is complaining – they're all nibbling away – and I can even read their minds: '*sure were all on bloody holidays – we'll worry about the old figure when we get home.*'

Two 'House Doubles' and two pints of 'Cisk' later, I'm feeling really at home. I'm chipping in to the banter at both sides of me, and really enjoying the fun. I could stay 'till closing time, but the old stomach reminds me that it can't operate on liquid alone, and I get a sharp longing for some real solid grub. I obey, and emptying my glass, prepare to go. But first, in my slightly inebriated joviality, I inform the whole bar of my leave-taking, bid farewell to all and sundry – complete strangers, as if I knew them all my life – and make my exit.

Another great plus for Roy's bar is that it's only a block from my hotel, and to really spoil me, the little walk is all down hill – important when you're a bit loaded and a little short of breath. In a flash I'm in the big restaurant, getting my usual warm welcome, and giving big bear hugs to my two favourite waitresses, Gladys and Marita.

I'm a bit late for dinner but that doesn't bother me, or bother the staff either. The big advantage of arriving towards the end is that I have the whole place to myself. Over a hundred tables free and waiting for me, and the affection and attention of charming Maltese beauties, relaxed now that the rush is over.

For a long time now, I have made a point of being a little late for dinner. At first I thought it might be a good idea

to arrive early when the doors opened at 5.45. but I soon banished that flawed brainwave – it was like a bloody Irish cattle fair.
What is it about being first for everything - especially dinner - that excites some British women? I just can't solve that puzzle. On the dot of 5.45, they seem to emerge out of cracks in the walls, followed sheepishly by obedient and acquiescing husbands or partners, and military style, prepare for a frontal assault. When the double doors open, they rush forward en masse in a great collective stampede – almost akin to 'The Charge of the Light Brigade' - or more accurately, '*Heavy Brigade.*'

Inside, still frenzied, they quickly take over. Tables are commandeered, claimed and reserved with handbags, room keys or bottles of wine, while they rustle to the buffet bar and form a queue that you jump at your peril - I find it hilarious. But it's also mysterious, because most of these ravenous Grannies are on 'All Inclusive' packages. This entitles them to breakfast, lunch, dinner, tea and coffee on demand, and a full bar service. No wonder most of them are top heavy, and have leg trouble from the excessive fluid and food intake, and the burden of weight carrying.

After packing in four courses of delicious grub, I'm now well fed and watered for this day, and feeling the pressure of a full belly, I ease myself out to the lounge where an assortment of guests are whiling away the evening. Some are sitting at tables scoffing cappuccinos, some are sipping pints of lager, and others are just sitting around watching TV - Sky News, of course. A few of the old ladies are busy multi-tasking – watching television, yapping away, and at the same time their hands and fingers are playing the knitting needles in a smooth rhythm as if on auto-pilot. I often wonder what drives them to do it – the fear of idle hands, or the need for some form of therapy.

I take a sweeping look around just in case any of my old buddies – *'partners in crime'* – are here, and at the same time, hoping that they are not - *tonight I need nourishment, not punishment.* The distant sound of music from the ballroom tells me that the dance is in full swing, and for a moment I'm tempted to head in that direction.

It's hard to beat this hotel for entertainment – live music and dancing every night, a swinging Night Club at weekends, and all the big football games shown on wide TV screens. Sure it's a bonanza of entertainment, and a massive temptation for a glutton for pleasure like myself.

I move out to the lobby and pause for thought. The lift doors are on my right, and the corridor leading to the ballroom is on my left. Decision time. Will I? Won't I? I defer to my better judgement and press the lift button. Soon I'm snug as 'a bug in a rug' ready for dreamland after a long, but interesting day.

****

Morning has Broken

As I explained, I like to be nearly last to evening dinner. In contrast, I'm one of the early birds to breakfast. Yes; you guessed it – I'm a morning person. I've always believed that for the first few hours from the crack of dawn, the air is cleaner, fresher, and far less polluted. Perhaps it's just a figment of my imagination - I don't know - but when I'm on my Maltese morning walks, I notice that the old legs are livelier, the head is clearer, and the old chest and lungs whistle less, and blow a lot easier. Yes, I'm convinced the air in Malta, especially the morning air, is premium stuff, a bonus that I greatly appreciate.

You see, I'm allergic to the old gloomy winter mornings in Ireland. I detest the thick fog, the incessant rain, the horrible dampness, not to mention the frost and snow, and the sky down on top of my head. No wonder I make my escape. Sure a morning's walk in Malta transforms the old body so much, that it's akin to putting aviation fuel in a car – puts a spurt in my tank - takes years off the old clock.

So, on my first full day here, I rise at six, shower, straighten myself up, skip my way down the eight flights of stairs – *lifts are for ascending* – through the dimly-lit

foyer, out through the revolving doors to the street, and savour a huge gulp of fresh Maltese air. It's an hour to breakfast time at half seven, the sky is cloudless, the head is surprisingly clear, so off I go to free up the old limbs, and soak in some of that beautiful scenery that for me makes this part of Malta extra special.
I need to cross over to the water side, as I want to skirt the shore all the way around Salina Point and down to St. Paul's Bay. Traffic is light, and as I'm crossing, I'm acutely aware of the life-threatening hazard this can be – even at this time of the morning. A fellow could be flung into oblivion if he wasn't careful. Maltese drivers are a terror. They're a law unto themselves. Young speed merchants are especially lethal. They roar past in noisy bangers, oblivious to the rules of the road, or any other users that may stray into their path. Light-flashing, roundabout manners and lane location, have a new meaning with these hell-drivers, and unfortunately, the many little roadside memorial shrines, dotted around the island, marking the spot of their sad demise, is testimony to the futility of their madness.

Much less hazardous are the many joggers I encounter along the way. Now, you know joggers come in all shapes and sizes, and in all levels of fitness. In Malta they are a particularly disparate lot. There's the elite – tanned, tight-skinned, hard-muscled, breezing past without a puff – the ones that really irritate me – *why can't I have a bloody body like that?* Then there's the semi-fit, overweight men and women, trying to emulate the elite, but their bodies just aren't up to it. They punish themselves, desperately trying to keep up a brisk, painful rhythm, while their faces indicate extreme suffering – I shouldn't speculate, but the words 'heart attack' and 'stroke' come to mind. And of course, there's always the 'shufflers.' These are grossly obese men – and even a few women - in their fifties and sixties who have for years gorged themselves with the goodies of life, and are now repentant and trying desperately to make reparation. You hear them before you see them. With their potbellies swinging from side to side, their breasts flopping in rhythm, and their lungs blowing like a bellows, they shuffle by at snail's pace. I look at them and I wonder; is it an act of madness or a form of suicide? For their own safety, I feel that, like the young joy-riders, they really should be banned from the roads.

I'm approaching the point of Salina Bay, the highest corner in Qawra, and the spot that, ten years ago, first grabbed my heart, causing me to swoon, and marvel at the absolute magic of the scenery. It's a vantage point to die for, giving a panoramic view of the bay, the loveliest basin of clear, blue Med water you'll ever see, and the creamy shoreline of Misra Bay and Xemxija, framing the background.

I'm now ready to inhale the beauty, but instead I'm stopped dead in my tracks by an eight foot wall of sheet steel cladding, extending so far down the road that I can barely see the end of it. What the hell is goin' on here? I just can't fathom out this monstrous thing that they have put up against me, robbing me of my glimpse of heaven. I can't see through it, over it, or under it, but hold on, I can hear heavy machinery revving up inside. Ah, they're building something. I walk on, mentally speculating until I come abreast with a massive hoarding looking down on the road, revealing all, and filling my head with even more questions.

A 'National Aquarium.' A joint venture between Marine Aquatic Ltd. and the Malta Tourism Authority. Cost 15 million euro – 49% funded by the EU – 43% funded by Marine Aquatic Ltd. – 15% funded by the Government of Malta.

'My God, thinks I – wonders will never cease!'

As I'm so absorbed in reading the small print, and still a bit hypnotised by the shock, I barely notice a stout little man approaching from the opposite direction leading four small dogs – two on each hand – small hairy things. As the footpath is now only half its normal width – the other halve is under *'The Great Wall of China'* – and with me planked in the middle, spellbound in my reading, the poor man has no alternative but to stop. I spot him and say sorry, but being the typical pleasant Maltese gentleman, he says, "No problem," and almost apologises himself for interrupting me.

We get chatting about the project, and as he lives close to it, he has done his homework, and has all the details at his fingertips.

"It's going to be huge," he says, "20,000 square metres, and apart from the aquarium, there will be a public garden, restaurants, and a two-storey underground car park. Twenty-six water tanks, some as big as twelve metres in diameter, will display a range of fish in

backdrops that will create the true feel of Malta's seabed."
"What kind of fish?" I ask, showing my complete ignorance of Maltese marine life.
He reels off an impressive list – many I had never even heard of – and then his face lights up.
"There's even going to be sharks in there, and they're planning to allow experienced divers to swim with them."

I can hardly believe what I'm hearing, and I'm wondering is this really Malta – or have I got my geography askew. This is a free lecture on aquatics by an expert to an imbecile, and I'm so interested and engrossed in it that I fail to notice what the four little upstarts are at below. In a casual peek down I realise they are having a ball at my trousers' expense. Both lower legs are now well and truly sprinkled with dog pee – the little piss-wiggers seem to be taking it in turns to direct the spray with pinpoint accuracy; getting great fun and relief.

The poor man is mortified and apologises profusely.
" Not a bother," I said, "sure 'tis only what little dogs do."
I thank him, and we head off in opposite directions – I, a better educated man, with wet trouser legs – him, still embarrassed by the misdemeanours of his little canine family.

I proceed briskly along the red paved walkway, enjoying the fresh morning breeze that is fanning my face and drying my pants. With no further monstrosity to obstruct my view, I fill my being with the beauty of the Mediterranean, as its clear blue waters meander in to greet me, gently kissing the rocky shoreline, and I'm almost tempted to step out into its freshness. I may do that later, but for now, I must complete this little trek, and be back in the hotel for early breakfast.

I'm past the massive Dolmen Hotel – it spreads like a giant mushroom over most of Bugibba – and now I'm approaching my little Eden. Bugibba Square has long been a special haunt for the Maltese, and especially for their guests. It's no bigger than a good-sized suburban back yard, but whatever it has got, it draws them, and in a couple of hours from now, it will be throbbing with activity and atmosphere.

For British tourists especially, this is the place to be, the hub that imbues the true magic of Malta, and the landmark that seems to connect all the surrounding locations in a little friendly centre circle. The quaint collection of little pubs, shops and cafe bars are still asleep, and the seats are bereft of bums, but for me the strange attraction is still there – I can feel it - and I'm nearly tempted to sit in, and claim squatters rights in this little haven of tranquillity. This little place always agrees with me. Many an hour I've spent relaxing here – snacking, reading, sitting and thinking, or just sitting – inhaling the leisurely ambience, the hot sun massaging my hide, the ocean smiling up at me, and I wondering what I ever did to deserve this heavenly lifestyle.

A picture of Bugibba Square would not be complete without the inclusion of a phenomenon that is not by any means unique to Malta – a pest for some, an opportunity for others: Timeshare salesmen. Of course there are saleswomen too, but in this little square, the men seem to rule the roost. For the ten years I've been coming here, the same half dozen slick, bronzed, and suave operators work the masses. Positioned at strategic entrance points, these hawk-eyed sharks can spot an elderly British couple approaching from a distance, and then, having firmly locked them on to their radar, track them until they arrive, greet them warmly, and hopefully seduce them into the wonderful world of 'timesharing.'

Now, I happen to know a little about the kind of skills needed for this work, and the special characteristics required. For many years I worked for a big international insurance company, and while seventy per cent of my work entailed servicing existing clients, the other thirty per cent involved the procurement of new prospects. I was entirely happy with the servicing, but I have to tell you, I detested the 'cold calling' needed to secure new clients. I just wasn't that kind of hard-necked, brazen predator, and that's why, when I watch these 'timeshare' wizards in action here, I must admit that they impress me with their tenacity and resilience, and I do have a sneaking admiration for them. And of course, they are well and truly part of the furniture here now, and their presence doesn't in any way spoil the pleasure and happiness this little square provides.

Before I leave Bugibba Square, I must mention something that often struck me here. Whoever planned and organised the seating, deserves 'top of the class'. A plentiful supply, well designed, and surprise, surprise, comfortable. They are positioned strategically to provide the best view of the bay, and at the same time, attract the most sun – a work of genius, I say, and an example for sure, that other resorts, with bigger egos and budgets, could well follow. Bravo! Whoever you are – take a bow!

On up the little incline, flanked on my left by a plethora of shops – mostly jewellery shops – and on my right by never-ending lines of eateries. I'm not sure what to call them - restaurants, cafes, takeaway's – but I am sure of one thing; the competition between them is fierce. Big colourful hoardings displaying their fare and their prices hit you as you pass, and I always marvel at the extent and variety of the menus on offer.

Full English breakfasts, toasts, rolls, sandwiches, wraps, burgers, baguettes, omelettes, salads, grills, pasta, chicken, fish, deserts, etc, etc. The list is endless, and of course, the prices are bargain basement. I sometimes wonder do they skimp on the quality or the quantity of the food, or else, do they manage to make a profit at all.

I'm double-tasking now – walking smartly and also admiring the view of St. Paul's Island across the sea to my right. Of course, as always, high on his plinth, on the little island rock, is the man himself. The Patron Saint of Malta, is gazing across at his beloved faithful, monitoring their every move, keeping them secure in the Christianity that he gave them two thousand years ago, a religious culture and devout piety, that they have preserved and cherished to this day.

As I skip over the brow, my eyes light up with the picture-postcard beauty that is St. Paul's Bay. Being mid-winter, the hundreds of little boats that usually crowd the bay, are now at home in dry dock. I miss them, especially the colourful little luzzus', Malta's unique craft, adorning the harbours, painted like works of art, and nurtured like treasured childhood toys. No doubt they will be back again in early spring, but for now all I can see is the myriad of little floating buoys attached to anchors, bobbing around, marking the spots that they vacated, and to where they will soon return.

I'm now down in the belly of St. Paul's Bay, and I must say it looks as picturesque and charming as ever. You may by now have guessed that this little area has always gripped me emotionally – I can't explain it, but as soon as I lower myself into its bowels, I'm a completely different animal, determined to change my ways, *turn over a new leaf,* and *'give up me oul sins'.* I'm in a haven of tranquillity, detached from the big bad outside world, mingling with angels and saints, and St. Paul himself organising everything.

Sure why wouldn't he? Didn't he struggle ashore at this very spot in 60 AD, shipwrecked on his way to Rome. And didn't he stay here for three months, being pampered and nourished by the natives, and in return for their goodness, he cured their sick, gave them the 'true faith', and pledged to protect and guide them for all time. That was surely a good bargain, and a fair one, and ever since, both Paul and the Maltese have faithfully adhered to the terms.

The little church that has marked the spot where he first set foot on the island still stands like a beacon in the square, reminding all-comers of that momentous moment of history, the miracle rescue of an execution-bound, future renowned saint, and the miraculous conversion of an island people. This ancient truth is so important that it was worthy of a chapter in no less a volume than the Holy Bible, and the Maltese are not shy in making the world aware of this distinction. The biblical reference is displayed in many languages on the perimeter walls of 'St. Paul's Shipwreck Church'.

I like attending mass in that little church - so small that at the *'sign of peace'*, all of the congregation can shake hands without moving out of their seats. It is certainly unique, and I have to say in all honesty, that I always experience a strange spirituality there, uplifting my soul with an injection of something, a mysterious stimulant that stays with me long after I've gone home.

Ten years ago when I first discovered St. Paul's Bay, I was captivated by its quaint charm and enchanted by its ancient history. I was much less impressed by the ramshackle state of its streets and buildings. Nothing appeared to have been touched since St. Paul's time and, although I could be wrong, perhaps that was the intention. Fair enough, but I'm a fellow that believes you can preserve the character and charm of a place and still keep it clean, tidy and respectable. However, year after year I returned undaunted, and every visit stirred in me those mixed emotions: rapture and awe as I melt into its spiritual bosom, and regret that it still had the derelict appearance, much of it sad, and suffering from neglect and decay.

Well, hello! This morning I'm elated. I just can't believe my eyes! The whole place is transformed – I can hardly recognise it. Posh new tarmac streets with dazzling white lines, perfectly paved new footpaths and kerbs, new elaborate, state of the art public toilets, beautiful wrought iron seats everywhere, street lamps that look like sculptures, and expensive-looking litter bins open for donations everywhere you look.

As I lovingly digest this feast of adornment, my eyes focus on the most impressive innovation of all: the construction of an elaborate system of decking stretching down along the shore. This viewing area and walkway extends out over the shoreline, and through the ingenious insertion of transparent grills, one can look down and monitor the activity below, as the Mediterranean flows gently in and out, caressing and massaging the smooth, time worn rocks.

This embellishment of an important medieval site could well have detracted from its ancient characteristics – I saw it happen before – but I have to say that, on the contrary, the whole redevelopment has been done with sensitivity and tender loving care. I'm not surprised – the EU were centrally involved – providing 85% of the cost, leaving the Malta government to cough up only 15%. That, in any language, is some deal, and all I can say is 'three cheers' for everyone involved – the EU, the government, and the craftsmen that excelled themselves with such beautiful work. Well done.

I'm almost at my turning point now, but first I must make a fleeting visit to a little inlet square nestling under the hill, that for me, is a real, genuine Maltese hamlet. All the apartments are inhabited by Maltese, their beautiful parish church is around the corner, and the little sheltered inlet is their swimming pool, their fishing grounds, and their oasis for sitting out in little groups, relaxing and chatting to their heart's content. This is the real Malta, and to-day it is dressed in its 'Sunday best' having been newly embellished as part of the overall St Paul's Bay redevelopment scheme.

I pause at the entrance to the little quay and wonder if my old friend Mella is around. I can't lay eyes on him – perhaps he's been down and gone home. I first met him in 2008, and as I was at that time, researching for my book, 'The Crying Sea' (The story of the Simshar fishing tragedy) he was invaluable to me, having been a fisherman himself. Since then, I have made a point of not leaving Malta without meeting him for a chat.

A real old-timer, now eighty-nine, he arrives down every morning at six with a plastic bag of bread to feed the twelve ducks that for many years have adorned the little dock. Many a morning, I've watched with fascination, as these graceful swimmers glide across from their home under the rocks, to meet Mella on the stroke of six, The joy they seem to radiate is also shared by Mella, as he exudes happiness and fun, seeing them so appreciative and vigorously competing for his goodies. Healthy and durable, living alone, Mella swims almost every day of the year, does a bit of fishing, and has, for an old fellow, surprisingly good English, which he generously uses to greet and converse friendly with intruders like myself – a pleasure that for me is always an uplifting experience. But alas, there's no sign of him today. I can see the ducks relaxing in the water, obviously bloated after scoffing Mella's breakfast - he's probably at home now having a bit of grub himself. So I turn, and with a hungry rumble in my belly, I leave St. Paul, and his idyllic little bay behind me, and head back for my own breakfast.

****

Our Daily Bread

I have found Malta to be a place that doesn't change much from year to year. The odd bit of tweaking; yes, but they don't go mad with wholesale reconstruction and modernisation as other countries do. Every year I look for changes and improvements, but the more I look, the more I see the same. Of course, I do find the odd block of apartments that I had observed taking years to snake up, suddenly become topped off – finished – done. I might see a new shop or two that wasn't there before, and maybe an old derelict corner given a new lease of life with some use or other – most likely an agency for 'Malta Highlights Tours' or some of the other tours that criss-cross the island.

Now, don't get me wrong; I'm not complaining, just noting the way they do things here. They go at their own pace, take their time, cut their cloth according to their measure, and if something or other has to wait a few years 'till they can afford it; then so be it – well and good. I would never argue with that – in fact, I totally agree.

You see, there's an awful lot to be said for that laid-back, prudent approach, and coming from Ireland, there's no one knows it better than me. Sure we went totally bonkers – completely lost the run of ourselves, went in no time, from boom to bust, ending up the bankrupt paupers we are today.

When the Irish and others were gorging on the cheap 'confetti' money being thrown at them by the ECB, and all the other banks, Malta said: "Hold on now, this might have to be paid back." They didn't lose their heads – saw through the folly of it all.
When we plastered our country with new, luxurious, state of the art homes, placed two limousines in the tarmac driveways, and embalmed ourselves with at least three sun holidays a year, the Maltese stuck with their age old dwellings, drove the same old dilapidated vintage cars, used their own sun to bronze themselves, and paid their way as they always did. The contagious greed that plagued most of Europe didn't contaminate Malta, they preserved their dignity and prosperity, while the others were sinking deep into the financial abyss of austerity and fiscal ruination.

Now, while millions of highly educated, bright young people across the continent are unemployed, banks and lending institutions are snowed under with repossessed houses and cars, suicides tragically increasing three-fold, and once great affluent countries being baled out with billions that their grandchildren will have to repay, Malta is happily coasting along without a care in the world, avoiding the fate of the other greedy vultures: recession, humiliation and ruin.

Now, I don't want to go on and on about this, but you'll have gathered that greed is a subject that can really fire my ire, unleash venom, and make my old temperature soar. It must have something to do with me being dragged up in the Ireland of the poverty-stricken fifties. You see, I had to learn the hard way about want and austerity – I can still feel the pain and I never want to see it again.

But the recent generations of the Irish never knew hunger or deprivation - they hadn't a clue – and that's why they foolishly believed that the 'gravy train' was an unstoppable machine, and the goose that laid the golden egg would live forever.

The really sad part of it is that we lost our way in other respects too. Affluence is a dangerous phenomenon. It can do strange things to a people. Our 'Land of Saints and Scholars' has now been renamed the 'Land of Crooks and Robbers'. I don't like the expression at all, but sadly, I have to admit, there's a grain of truth in it.

We certainly have lost our friendliness, our good manners, and our neighbourliness – old Irish characteristics renowned the world over. Malta is so different. I can never see them discarding their cherished values: honesty, integrity, warmth, charity and sincerity, qualities that for me are always greatly admired, and very much appreciated.
Retracing my steps back around Salina Point, the 'Wavecrest Hotel' suddenly appears and stares at me from the distance. It has an immediate effect on my

empty stomach, causing it to send signals to my other organs – weak legs, dry mouth and a distinct rashers-like smell to my nostrils. Giving the watch a cursory glance, I realise that my little walk has taken half an hour longer than usual, and now of course, the gang of eccentrics that I had expected to reunite with, will have finished stuffing themselves, and gone about their day's activities.

Not so. As I tentatively descend the marble steps and enter the lounge leading to the restaurant I'm set upon by a little animated welcoming party that almost sweep me off my feet. Now, you may not have guessed it, but I'm basically a shy lad – always have been – and I'm the last person in the world to encourage or relish an exuberant and boisterous welcome – I hate being made a fuss of – but when you're associating with a posse of tricksters like these, you have no chance at all – just go with the flow.

The three of them have set themselves up at a table directly inside the lounge door, and like members of the 'Special Branch,' have been monitoring all entrants until they finally captured their prey. I should have figured that news of my return would have been leaked to them by the waitresses from last night, but it never crossed my mind - another sign of the old brain diminishing with age. Anyway, they were ready to pounce, and as they are by now well acquainted with my morning timetable, their ambush was perfectly timed and executed. Applause, cheers, hand shakes, bear hugs, kisses – I had to endure the lot, and as *they* now had full bellies, they were in no hurry to release me to the restaurant – much to my tummy's exasperation.

The undisputed leader of the pack is a scoundrel by the name of Len from Essex. No more than eight stone, a jockey-like figure, groomed to the last, impeccably dressed, smart as a bee – nobody would believe he was eighty-three. A widower living alone, he is the comic entertainer of the 'Wavecrest' – *some would say the 'bane' of their vacation* – from Christmas to March when he returns to his dainty cottage, his Mercedes, and his self-sufficient vegetable garden. What a life, and Len lives it to the full.

Second in command is Charlotte from Birmingham, a tall, slim attractive fifty-something – she only gives her birthday, not her birth date – divorced, single, and readily available for fun, adventure, or 'whatever your having yourself'. She is another perfect example of the type that Oscar Wilde had in mind when he uttered his famous quote: *"Can resist everything except temptation*". She is a regular here – comes and goes – a glutton for pleasure, a joking and laughing machine, and a breath of fresh air to moody sods like myself that are sometimes inclined to wallow in gloom or self-pity.

Then there's Trevor from Manchester, about sixty, low stocky build with magnifying glasses, single, living alone, comes here for three months every year. I suppose in every group there has to be variety. That's where Trevor fits in. He is the quiet one, droll, laid-back, timid, but witty, cunning, and never misses a chance to be involved in whatever mischievous schemes the others might be up to.

So you see, if I include myself, this is a gang of carefree bohemians, free spirits and life-lovers, harmless enough individually, but lethal collectively, always ready, willing and able for any adventurous assignments that Malta may dish up.

We move to a quieter, traffic-free zone in the far corner of the lounge and, like a football team before kick-off, we huddle together in an exchange of tittle-tattle, a colourful account of the life and times of London, Birmingham, Manchester and Ireland over the past year. Sure it's as good as any news round-up or magazine programme ever broadcast on the BBC or Sky. We cover all aspects of human life, and although my head is now stuffed with an abundance of food for thought – much of it suspect – my guts are growling for some real tangible grub. I cut to the chase, turn the debate to the subject of breakfast, and on the solemn pledge that I would join them this evening in the ballroom, I'm reluctantly released to the succour of the restaurant.

Breakfast in the 'Wavecrest' can be whatever you want it to be – within reason, of course, Champagne and Caviar are not yet on the menu – but if you can't appease whatever kind of finicky appetite you have, it's entirely your own fault. The grub is all there, buffet style, and nobody takes a bit of notice of the number of visits you make to the counter, or the volume of grub that you shovel into yourself.

The buffet is a great idea, but as we all know, it's like shopping in a massive supermarket; once you get started, it's hard to know when to stop. Take me for example. I have been known to make an old sow of myself and gobble up three or four courses. Once I get the snout in the trough, I won't stop 'till I'm stuffed and inflated like a 'Michelin Man'. But in all honesty, that's now the exception for me, and it's usually the consequence of some occurrence that may have upset me. Comfort eating they call it, and sure there's not a lot wrong with that if it relieves some little hurt or other.

But seriously, I have to tell you, All my life I'm plagued with a metabolism that says: if *you* only smell food, you'll put on weight, and if you put something in your mouth that tastes nice and sweet, spit it out quick; it's bad for you. So you can see the tightrope I've been walking - food is my God – not only do I have a sweet tooth, I have a whole mouthful of them. And of course, the 'demon drink', with it's potent, belly-enlarging properties, should be a complete no-go area for me, but sure what would I do then? – join some 'order' and become a real hermit. It's a struggle for a comfort freak like me, and a never-ending test of discipline. But I must say that by and large, I have managed to keep the old sow in me under control. I'm fine when everything in my garden is rosy, but if the old head is bothered about something, it soon transfers to the guts, and there's only one remedy then: food, glorious food.
This is one morning that I feel like indulging – I think I've earned it - but I promise I'll be a good lad and avoid

the goodies from tomorrow on – *'famous last words'*. I hit the cereal counter. A good helping of muesli topped off with fresh fruit cocktail, smothered with yogurt and some honey will do nicely for the first course. It's just delicious. I'm tempted to lick the plate, but the waiter is at my side, ready to pounce. What is it about waiters that they are allergic to empty vessels on a table? This restaurant seats five hundred people, divided into six sections, giving the waiter assigned to each section about twenty tables. I can never figure out how, with a cursory glance, they are able to monitor the progress of each diner, arrive in the nick of time to grab the plate as the last morsel has been consumed. It's an art, but I still can't get my head around it.

Now, you won't be surprised to hear that as an Irishman, I have always loved a big fry-up for breakfast – have you ever met one yet that didn't? – but my doctor kept telling me to "throw that bloody pan out the window", and he wasn't shy in using strong-arm tactics to force me. I resisted for a while – quoting Oscar Wilde's theory: *"Convince a man against his will – and he remains unconvinced still"*, but when he assured me that I would end up with high cholesterol, angina, diabetes, stroke, heart attack, etc, etc – you name it – I was destined for it – reluctantly, I had to relent.

Today, I'm banishing all that to the back of my head as I load my plate with three sausages, three rashers, two fried eggs, a large mound of scramble and a generous helping of succulent beans. Balancing all that in one hand and a plate of toast, butter and marmalade in the other, and reach my table intact, is a feat more suitable for a juggler, but I manage it, and I must say it all looks gorgeous and appetising in front of me.

The thing about a big restaurant with hundreds of tables is that you can usually find one in a position that is agreeable, a handy spot that provides a vantage point to oversee the spectacle of feeding time for the masses. When I first came here I sampled a few different locations, and having found some little disadvantage in each, I finally settled on a table in a quiet corner far away from the entrance door and the buffet counter. This allowed me the security of having my back to the wall, the privacy of feeding alone in my own unrefined way without prying eyes following my every mouthful, and the fascination of studying the various idiosyncrasies of all the other diners – an exercise that can be informative as well as highly entertaining. I'm now known as 'Jack in the Corner,' a title lovingly bestowed on me by my waitress friend Mirana - it doesn't bother me at all; in fact I rather like the little dubious distinction.

Anyway, I'm munching away to my heart's content, and I suppose it's because I'm extra hungry this morning that I'm paying little attention to the other diners, or for that matter, to the flavour and quality of the grub I'm shovelling into my mouth. I always find that when I'm stuffing myself to ease my hunger pangs, anything remotely edible will do, but as I'm getting topped up, I get all picky and find fault with everything. In fairness now, I really can't complain much about this plate of 'forbidden fruit' except that the rashers are more cremated than grilled, and the flavour of the slim-line sausages is non-existent, and bear no resemblance to the big jumbos that I relish back home whenever I lapse from my fry-abstinence, and have a 'full Irish'.

I'm getting loaded now and, having slowed down, I'm beginning to notice that there are other diners here apart from myself. They don't rush the doors in the early morning as they do for evening dinner. There's a trickle at first, it rises to an influx about halfway through, and eases off again towards the end. One thing that intrigues me is this: why do the British not trust the Maltese to wash cups? Plates, bowls, glasses, cutlery, yes - but cups, no. It seems to be a serious matter for them – so serious that they can't afford to take a chance. So the women amble in to the restaurant with a handbag in one hand and a mug in the other. Not only that, but the men follow sheepishly behind, and yes, you guessed it, armed with a mug too.

Now, I've tried to get a 'handle' on this – if you pardon the pun – but as yet, I've failed. Lets look at it this way. If it were a case of the restaurant cups being too small, fair enough, but I'm certain that with the appropriate representation to the 'Food and Beverage' manager, suitable larger ones could easily be provided. No, it's something else. I'm convinced it's all in the mind. I suspect that they have these horror visions of all the disease-ridden wretches that have supped from those cups in the past, and they're determined to avoid any semblance of a germ, dead or alive, that the Maltese in their negligence may have failed to remove. It reminds me of a tried and trusted old Irish motto: *better be safe than sorry.*

Another thing that impresses me about the British diners – particularly the women – is their ability to consume a hearty breakfast, and at the same time make provision for essential snacks to fill a gap later, when they might expect to feel a bit peckish. It's a clever little technique that they have perfected, and the dexterity is so fine-tuned, that the waiters have no chance to detect it. But from years of close observance, I can now see clearly how it's done – and it's really quite simple.

They get their breakfast plate, make a counter attack, load up the plates to full capacity, but in addition to the usual breakfast fare, they pile up bread, cheese, cold meat and crackers – ostensibly for immediate consumption – but when back at the table they commence their ingenious multi-task routine. Keeping one eye on the waiter, pretending to be eating their breakfast normally, they are busy wrapping the little packs in serviettes, and with deft hand movements – worthy of any stage magician – the goodies miraculously transfer to the handbags.

As I say, I now know how it's done, but for the life of me, I can't fathom why it's done. It's hardly to save money, although with some of those long-stay guests it could add up to a tidy sum. My suspicion is that they derive some little inner pride and satisfaction for having the ability to hoodwink the poor innocent waiters - a bit like a shoplifter feels having performed a successful 'killing.' It has to be motivated by some adventurous impulse, because it is all done in blatant defiance of a clear message from the management, displayed prominently over the buffet counter.

DEAR GUEST
PLEASE DO NOT REMOVE FOOD FROM THE RESTAURANT
ANY FOOD TAKEN OUT WILL BE CHARGED TO YOUR ACCOUNT.
THANK YOU.

I wonder over the years, how many accounts have been debited? Your guess is as good as mine.

I could do with a strong coffee now to wash down that greasy grub and pep me up with some stimulating caffeine. That's one little gripe I have with this restaurant – beverage dispensing machines. Now, I am, and have been for years, a coffee addict - I could drink ten a day – but like everything else that I fancy; it's bad for me. So I limit my intake now to three – morning, noon and night. That's why I'm choosy when it comes to quality. I like a good, strong, nicely flavoured cuppa, and I detest the coloured water those machines pee out. I have to concede though, that this machine here is not the worst I've seen. It's modern and has the welcome feature of a button that sends out a gush of strong expresso. So I make the most of it by pressing the button three times, filling my cup to the brim with a strong, caffeine-loaded potion, that will keep me fortified and sustained till midday.

On my way out through the lounge, I notice I'm not as agile or free moving as I was coming in, but sure that little impediment is only temporary, no real burden, and a small price to pay for a full belly, and a lovely warm feeling of contentment.

****

Out and About

One of the lessons I have learned from long experience is that for anyone like myself on a long-stay vacation – with no company except my own – it is imperative to have a plan for each day, and for each hour to be filled with planned activity of some kind, however trivial. This is a self-imposed rule that I've always tried to adhere to, and it has kept me sane, civil, and satisfied, protecting me from boredom, depression, and those sudden, sulky impulses to 'throw in the towel' and look up the next Ryanair flight home.

I've long believed that having nothing to do and all day to do it, is a recipe for all sorts of weird, unidentifiable, human conditions, and a formula for the conception of mind games that, if allowed to develop and play out, could spell disaster, and make a confused hash of an otherwise sensible intellect. So, when I'm in Malta I practice what I preach, to the extent that my hours and days are so full, that you couldn't really say I'm on a holiday or a vacation at all. You couldn't really call it work either, rather more accurate to describe it in the words of an old Irish expression: *'I'm living the life of Reilly'.*

After breakfast, fed and watered for the day, I return to my room for a bit of relaxation, a chat with myself regarding the rest of the day, a spot of domestic tidying-up, and all the while being updated on the state of the world from the BBC World News. For years I have been watching momentous international events unfold through a haze of snow on an ancient little black box hanging precariously high up on the wall of my room, not knowing when it as going to blow up or crash down. Thankfully, it did neither, and now, surprise, surprise, I arrive, elated to find a gleaming new 'flat screen' showing me the world in the most vivid clarity, and being sensibly positioned at eye level, saving me from that painful nuisance; the crick in the neck.

I've always been a nut for tidiness. At home I swear by the old motto: *'a place for everything and everything in its place'*. I suppose living alone does that to you. My late mother drummed it into us too, and *her* motto was: *'if you don't mess it up, you won't have to clean it up.'* Great logic in that. Here in Malta I'm the same, making sure the room is always in shipshape, and gloating on the thought of how impressed the cleaning lady would be when she arrives to find it sparkling, almost akin to it being unoccupied. It's crazy, I know, but I can't help it; that's me.

But I do see some sense in it too. I can well imagine what two ravenous lovers – especially on a sex-filled vacation - can do to a bed and a room over the course of a long steamy night, and with the greatest sympathy for the loyal band of room cleaners, who have to face the aftermath, at least my celibacy and tidiness will give one of them a break.

I'm ready for the road. First stop is the Internet Café in down town Bugibba, a stretch of Tourist Street full of souvenir shops, bars, restaurants, hairdressers, chemists, and a couple of well-stocked supermarkets. My whole world now revolves around the Web. At this stage I've given up trying to solve the mystery of how we managed to live our lives before the advent of this wonderful and life-changing phenomenon. The world is now literally before our eyes and at our fingertips, and millions of people, scattered all over the planet, are now connected in a vast togetherness, that is almost too marvellous to comprehend.

Malta is well served with strong, fast broadband, and with the youth all well educated, and as technically literate as in most other countries, they are equipped with a myriad of gadgets to receive it. It is also now available in the larger hotels, and the internet cafés sprouting up all over the island are an expanding and lucrative business.

But here is the snag. Not everywhere will you find the machines up to the job. I know it's early days and things will definitely improve, but there's such a vast difference in performance, and they all cost the same, that you really would want to go on a fact-finding mission before squandering your money on a sham that will neither reward you or refund you, leaving you with the worst form of frustration.

Last year on my arrival in the 'Wavecrest,' I was proudly informed that they had now installed their own Wi Fi, and it was accessible in all the bedrooms. Well, was I thrilled? – I thought all my birthdays had come together. I had visions of sitting at my desk, luxuriating in the comfort, privacy, and freedom of my room, connecting with the world, uploading and downloading at any hour of the day, or even in the dead of night if I fancied it – magic, just magic!

But of course, the sting was in the tail. It didn't come cheap. You pay ten euro for a ticket, giving you six hours of surfing, you set up the laptop, enter the code and bingo, you're in heaven. The cost didn't bother me unduly. I was happy to pay for this wonderful facility, connecting my own little room to the big wide world, just as if I was back home in my little office surfing away to my heart's content – as the saying goes: *'happy as a pig in shit'*.

But alas, I have to tell you, it was all a dream – no, a bloody nightmare. For two fraught days I experimented with it, I battled with it, I pleaded with it, I cajoled it, I cursed it, and in the end I was so exasperated that my little loyal laptop took the brunt of my anger, and by some miracle or the grace of God, was 'saved by the bell' from being hurtled out the window to be smashed in smithereens on the pavement below.

On the point of conceding defeat, and desperately nagging the old head to come up with some brainwave, to either rescue the situation or suggest an alternative, my old friend 'Fate' stepped in again. Suddenly, through the haze of my despair, this lovely new snooker hall and internet café appeared out of nowhere, and as they say: the rest is history. The machines are obedient, fast and frugal, and for two Euro, I can spend an hour each morning wandering the exciting superhighway of cyberspace, visiting my websites, updating my blogs, researching in its vast encyclopaedia, keeping myself abreast of things in Ireland, via the Irish Times, and organising my financial and personal affairs, leaving me happy and contented, and more certain than ever that there really is a God up there.

Back to earth again after my rewarding travels in cyberspace, I celebrate with a nice cap of Twinings English tea, and vacate the café. The day is bright, the sky is blue, and the sun is beaming down its soothing rays, so I go next door for a paper, and then amble across the street to the Dolman Garden, where my bench is already heated and waiting to receive my bum. So, for the next hour I'll be the most contented man alive, resting the bones, acquiring a few extra freckles, scouring the 'Times of Malta' for all the news of the day, and completing the crossword – an essential exercise to keep the old brain lubricated. Oh, I know, it's a tough old life, but sure someone has to do it.

Malta has a good range of newspapers, most of which are in Maltese. The two English language ones are 'The Times' and 'The Independent,' both excellent, particularly 'The Times,' which is bigger, more comprehensive, and featuring a wider range of comment and analysis.

I've grown so used to 'The Times' now that I feel my day wouldn't be complete without it, and even when I'm back home in Ireland, I make a point every morning of reading it on the Internet. I've also studied the history of this famous newspaper, and it has certainly earned its widely recognised status as a true 'national institution'. Founded 7th August 1935, it has never missed a day since, and during World War 11, all through the terrible bombardment of Malta, when more bombs fell here than on the city of London, the founders and staff courageously struggled on through the mayhem, and miraculously got the paper out to its besieged readers, and have been rewarded ever since with an appreciative and loyal readership.

Of course, the island is awash with British newspapers. They are all here, tabloids and broadsheets, and as the English love their newspapers – 'rags' would be a more accurate description of some of them – they are flown in every morning, displayed outside almost every shop, and snapped up by the scandal-hungry, and homesick British. They're welcome to them, as far as I'm concerned. They can enjoy the silly, suggestive headlines and the page three titillations, I'll stick to my 'Times' and keep my mind out of harm's way.

Having used up my pleasant hour on the bench, I rise, nicely rested, fully informed of Malta's good and bad news, and a bit peeved with my brain for having failed to give me the solution to one crossword. My usual proficiency as a wordsmith has lured me to assume a bit of an ego where crosswords are concerned, and, like Humpty Dumpty, it suffers a great humiliating fall when some smart Alec, like the crossword setter in the 'Times', baffles and defeats me. It's happened again today, and it's not pleasant. But sure, worse could happen – I'll just have to grin and bear it.

I'm back on Tourist Street and browsing the shops as I amble along in the direction of my hotel. This is one of the big tourist areas of Malta, with lots of multi-roomed hotels, self-catering accommodation, and thousands of flats and apartments – many of them so ugly and unsightly, that I often wonder how they ever got planning permission. Although the cuisine in the 'Wavecrest' is agreeable enough to me, I still like to meander around the shops and supermarkets to get a 'flavour' of the food on offer, and to compare it with Ireland. Food is certainly big business here. You can imagine the thousands of people in those apartments and other accommodations that self-cater, and have to shop every day, especially for fruit and vegetables, that wouldn't last long in this climate. I have to concede that, by and large, the shops and supermarkets are excellent, well-stocked, and in true Maltese friendliness, succeed in that most problematic assignment, pleasing all the customers.

Before I leave the subject of food, I really have to tell you of a discovery I made in the early days of my exploration of Malta. Back in the Ireland of the forties and fifties, when I was a school-going nipper, the Ireland of bare feet, yellow porridge, and dry bread, when poverty was rife and families like ours were on the brink of starvation, one small animal came to our rescue: the little bunny rabbit. The land was overrun with them, and the farmers were tearing their hair out trying to eradicate them, or at least curtail their appetite for lovely young green crops.

Now, everyone knows that rabbits make great pets, but I suspect they make great lovers too, because at the rate they were populating the land of Ireland in those days, their love-making must have been never-ending. Well, for us chaps, in dire need of a few pennies to jingle in the pockets of our multi-patched trousers, they couldn't breed fast enough. For us it was a number's game – a dozen snares, set properly, would yield at least four rabbits, and at one and sixpence each, that was manna from heaven. Not only did it put a jingle in our pockets, but it also greased our mother's magic purse, and sustained us all with the best of organically-fed rabbit meat.

What has all that got to do with Malta? It's a legitimate enough question, and I'll answer it like this. In the Ireland of fifty years ago, the little rabbit was the poor man's 'steak' – it was probably as good as any steak – but it was still seen as a last resort, rescue remedy, sent by God to save the poverty-stricken from utter starvation. Now, can you imagine my amazement when I happened to ramble in to an up-market meat shop here one day, just having a gape around to see the kind of meat the Maltese eat, to find, displayed and given pride of place, my little childhood benefactor, the bunny rabbit.

Rows of them hanging naked on hooks over the counter, respected and cherished as a prime delicacy, and commanding the premium price. Well, I must say, I was astonished, but also delighted to see our little friend, that kept us alive and fortified with childhood energy all those years ago, was now at last elevated to princely status in a far distant land. Well, says I, my little friend, you have come a long way, and as the old folks in Ireland would say: *'it's a long road that has no turn'*.

I must mention fish too, because being an island, fishing and fish have for centuries been synonymous with Malta. The Mediterranean is rich with an abundance of various species, and the Maltese fishermen are adept at catching them. On my frequent visits to many of the excellent fish shops dotted around the island, and as a lover of most fishy dishes, I am always captivated by the range and quality of the fish on display, from the tiniest shellfish to the majestic tuna and swordfish, and in between those handsome gems of the Med, awrat, shnott and lampuki. The most astonishing range of fresh fish I have ever seen can be viewed in what I regard as the best fish shop in Malta: Azzopardi Fisheries, only a 'stone's throw' from my hotel, and where I love to savour that unique fresh fish aroma as I pass it every day. Not only are all the local 'catch' displayed and promoted, but on perusal of the massive display counter, I have found Baby Sise from Italy, Neonati from China, Prawns from Venezuela and Argentina, Cernia from Holland and Garnet from

Morocco, among a myriad of other exotic species from around the world. What a selection! What a choice. Fair play to Anthony Azzopardi for his initiative and enterprise.

Fishing, as most would agree is an ancient craft that is traditionally handed down from generation to generation. It takes courage, patience, tenacity and resilience, but every fisherman I ever knew – and Ireland has thousands of them – lives for fishing, and even in periods of the bleakest drought, they would still persevere, and the thought of doing any other job would never cross their minds.

It can also be fraught with danger and disaster – in Ireland we lost three boats and a dozen fishermen in the past three years. Malta, for all its fishing activity has been relatively lucky over the years. A bad storm cost the lives of fishermen way back in 1924, but for the following eighty-four years, by some miracle source of protection, not one boat or life was lost. Sadly, that all changed in July 2008, when a fishing tragedy occurred that rocked the nation, caused unspeakable anguish for the crew; shock, horror and grief for the Island of Malta.

It was one of the most intriguing sea mysteries of recent times, and how or why it happened is as yet unclear. According to the sole survivor, an explosion and fire sank the 'Simshar', throwing her crew into the Mediterranean, and the island of Malta into shock and devastation. Three years has now passed since the tragedy, but the Maltese people are still confused and bewildered. They are baffled and unconvinced with the explanations offered, and the scant evidence produced to show what really happened on that ill-fated voyage.

On Monday 7th July 2008, at around 5 am, Simon Bugeja, the skipper of the fishing vessel 'Simshar' left the port of Marsaxlokk for a swordfishing trip, eighty miles from Malta, near the island of Sicily. Also on board the vessel were his 61-year-old father, his eleven-year-old son, Theo, a 33-year-old Maltese crewman, and a 19-year-old Somalia crewman. Five days later, Sharon Bugeja, (wife of skipper Simon) reported the vessel missing. The Armed Forces of Malta embarked on a search and rescue operation, but despite the massive air and sea search, scanning the Mediterranean for six days, they found no trace of the vessel or its crew.

On Friday 18th July 2008, Simon Bugeja (the skipper) was found alive on a makeshift raft by the fishing vessel, 'Gracale', 59 miles west south west of Malta. He was in an appalling physical condition, and near to death. The skipper told how on Thursday 10th July, an explosion and fire destroyed the 'Simshar'. All their lifesaving equipment was lost, they had no means of sending a distress signal, and were left clinging to a makeshift raft without food or water. He recounted the eight days of horror as the crew perished one by one, and sank to the depths of the ocean. His most heart-wrenching description was the graphic portrayal of his brave little son, cradled in his arms, on a flimsy raft, without food or water, for eight harrowing days and nights, battling to stay alive in the hope of being rescued. Miraculously, father and son kept each other alive far beyond normal endurance limits, but for little Theo, it was not long enough, he died on the eve of the arrival of the rescue boat, and in the darkness of the night slipped from his father's arms, into the heart of the Mediterranean.

But what really happened to the 'Simshar'? What is the true story of the first fishing disaster that Malta has suffered since 1924? In its aftermath, the island was awash with rumour and innuendo, raw anger, inflamed by incredible conspiracy theories, and widespread reports of Maltese and Sicilian fishermen at war. The Maltese government was forced to act. Two official inquiries were set up: a preliminary Marine Department Investigation, and a full-blown Police Inquiry. Would they unearth the truth?
The sole survivor, Skipper, Simon Bugeja, has told his story, outlining the sequence of events that led to the tragic shipwreck, and his crew's desperate struggle for survival. His testimony is taken on face value, but huge questions remain unanswered. There is no independent evidence to corroborate his account of what happened.
While researching my novel, 'The Crying Sea', - which recalls the tragedy - I have spent many days among the fishermen in the little port of Marsazlokk, the home of the 'Simshar,' and the Bugeja family, discussing the tragedy, and hearing their considered views of how and why it may have happened. There are still many doubts in my mind regarding the whole tragic episode. The Marine Department enquiry has reported, but having read its 140 pages, I am none the wiser, as it could not find any new evidence to confirm or deny the skipper's

account. Perhaps the Police Inquiry, following three years of probing, will soon report with credible answers that will bring closure to this sad and intriguing saga.

***

I have always been an zealous timekeeper. I honestly believe that there's some kind of clock in my head that sets my daily timetable, monitors my every move, adjusts the speed and timing of all my routines, and punishes me with a horrible guilt feeling when my old body doesn't obey, and I'm lagging behind in my schedules. Even when I'm asleep, it continues its vigilance, waking me on the dot of whatever time I had mentally intended before going to bed. Don't get me wrong, I'm not complaining. In fact, I'm very grateful to have such a handy apparatus on my person – one of the few bright sparks of an otherwise mediocre brain.

So, I arrive back at the hotel on the stroke of one, glide into the lobby through the revolving doors, turn right into the 'Café Grande,'and plonk myself down by a table in a quiet corner, where I can enjoy the sun, study the activities of the other diners, and soak up the special ambience of this haven of comfort and tranquillity. Of all the cafés that I've frequented over the years, I haven't come across another one to top the 'Café Grande.' It is part of the 'Wavecrest', occupying a large slice of the ground floor, and with its unique pavement annex, forms a seamless harmony between the hotel and the street.

It was obviously designed to exude warmth, charm and personality, and I'm always impressed to see how admirably it succeeds in achieving that ambition. The glorious décor, with its clever placement of diamond-cut mirrors and gleaming brass fittings, the elegant furniture, crafted and designed for maximum comfort and co-ordination, the clever use of soft, discreet lighting, the perfusion of indoor plants and greenery, the staff, regally suited, ever friendly and efficient, the menu, a work of art, and the cuisine, a feast of mouth-watering specialities, normally reserved for once-off occasions, but here, an everyday treat.

It's a café of the old style, a relic of old fashioned grandeur, a survivor from the good old days of taste and quality, and a fitting legacy to the Macallef Brothers – now sadly passed on – for their vision to conceive and successfully create this two-tier concept of a highly modern facility of comfort and relaxation, and at the same time preserving its character, elegance and the old world charm of bygone days.

I order a Tuna and Spinach Pie, a Café Latte, and settle down to an hour of relaxing pleasure, enjoying not only the food, but also the close observance of the other diners, as they bloat themselves with an array of luxurious confectionery of truly epic proportions. Now, I know you're going to conclude that I'm nothing short of a mischievous rascal, because of my sneaky habit of sitting in a restaurant or café, ostensibly feeding myself and minding my own business, when in reality, I am, by stealth, taking pleasure and entertainment from innocent diners, doing their own thing, oblivious to the mirth and comedy they are unwittingly providing. But honestly, I don't feel a bit guilty at all, for if, in the privacy of my own simple mind, I'm enjoying a little 'side show', where's the harm in that? – it's a victimless crime – and who's to say that this hulk here is not the secret laughingstock of my fellow diners too. *Stranger things have happened.*

Anyway, the café is humming, the clientele is a mixture of tourists from the 'Wavecrest', other hotels and accommodations, and a good sprinkling of Maltese, who I know, adore their 'Black Forest', 'Chocolate Fudge', and 'Knickerbocker Glory', especially the classic creations of the 'Café Grande.'

There was an EU study done recently, measuring the obesity levels of the inhabitants of all twenty-seven countries. In announcing the result to you, I should really have a fanfare – a bit like the 'Oscars' – ***And the winner is:*** England! ***And the second is:*** Malta! Oh, I know I shouldn't gloat, Ireland finished well up in the top ten. But I'm really not surprised at all. What I see in front of me now, is a clear vindication of those study results. There are English and Maltese diners here, of enormous proportions, akin to 'Ten Ton Tessies' and Oliver Hardy's, and they're scoffing away to their enlarged heart's content, on gooey, calorie-laced cakes and gateaux, and I'm sure their voracious consumption of this weight-enhancing fuel is a joyous experience for them, but I wonder is it wise? and is it a good exchange for the inevitable shortening of their lives. It's really no laughing matter, and I'm no 'Twiggy' myself, but if I was as ballooned as some of those unfortunates, I think I would certainly cop on.

Anyway, I've had enough – eating, observing, ranting – so with an aura of smug righteousness, this perfect specimen of manhood, this epitome of discipline and self-denial, relinquishes the den of indulgence to the gluttons, and returns to the safe haven of his bedroom. I reward myself with a little nap to recharge the batteries, and freshen up the old brain, before embarking on a little spot of scribbling.

***

It was a weird twist of fate, back in the eighties, that got me started in this writing game, at a time when I was quite long in the tooth, and certainly no spring chicken. But it was a God-send, because, as the young brood were leaving the nest to broaden their horizons, I was finding extra free time, and smelling around for something to do with it. A number of extra curricular activities and pursuits began to attract my attention - golf, photography, travel, etc. – but writing books didn't even form a minuscule speck in the mind or the imagination. Of course, I was always an avid reader, and although I loved and admired all the literary icons like Hemingway, Yeats and Wilde; that was it. It never crossed my mind that one day, I might dabble in it myself.

It was one of those miserable winter evenings, and in the warmth of the house, I was passing the time browsing my local weekly newspaper. A tiny advertisement, caught the corner of my eye, and having turned the page, it refused to vacate my vision. Reverting back, I read that it was announcing a 'Creative Writing Course,' starting the following week in the community hall of our local village. Something about it pricked my imagination, forcing me to read it a few times. Isn't it amazing how these things emerge out of the blue, commandeer your brain, and for no logical reason, trigger impulsive decisions that can change your life. I was convinced, there and then, without a shadow of a doubt, that this was for me, and the answer to my ongoing search for whatever it was that I was looking for. It reminded me of the old truism; *I don't know what I'm looking for, but when I find it, I'll know.*

Anyway, without a second thought, I picked up the phone, rang the number, verbally enrolled, and having replaced the receiver, took a deep breath, and asked myself: what possessed you to do that? I turned up on the day, to find myself in the company of two other men – both retired – an assortment of six women of various ages, shapes and sizes, and an attractive young tutor, that didn't look a day over twenty-five. We sat around a large table with pens and paper at the ready, anxiously awaiting our gentle introduction to the basic mechanics of writing. I, for one, hadn't a clue what to expect. But we were in for a bit of a shock, a beginning that no one expected, it jerked us out of our complacency, and concentrated our minds.

With a mischievous smirk on her face, our shapely mentor planted a large brass candlestick on the centre of the table with the order: "I want you all to write a page of prose about this". Well, everyone stared wide-eyed at each other, and judging by the looks of apprehension it was obvious that we were all on the same rung of the literary ladder – the bottom one. Write about a candlestick! Was this for real, or a joke to lighten up the atmosphere? No, it wasn't a joke. We had to do it, and when all was completed, and after the compulsory read-out, I got the gist of what our clever tutor was about. It was a master stroke - an early appraisal for her of the aptitudes and abilities of this motley crew, and for us the clearest possible glimpse into what creative writing was all about.

It was the dead of winter, and although at times we collectively shivered in the ice-cold hall, we stuck it out – one day per week for ten weeks – received our certificates at the end, and went our separate ways. I can't vouch for the others, but for me, it was just magic. Looking back on it now, ten published books later, I'm eternally grateful to 'Fate', or whatever abstract phenomenon inspired me on that winter's evening. It was my passport to heavenly bliss, and I often wonder since, what did I ever do to deserve it?.

****

It takes all kinds

In their enlightened design of the 'Wavecrest,' the Macallef Brothers saw the benefit of including a large modern ballroom, that would hold at least a thousand people, and they duly provided it. Although the Brothers are no longer here, the breadth of their vision is clearly evident in this beautiful rendezvous of pleasure and carefree abandon. It is also a lucrative source of additional revenue for the hotel as, in addition to the nightly dance – boosting bar sales - many other functions are held throughout the week, bringing large numbers of Maltese for conferences, celebrations, parties and bingo sessions. As is well recognised, the Maltese are devout Catholics, and every Sunday, the furniture is rearranged and it becomes a church, when an elderly retired priest celebrates Mass on the stroke of mid-day, attended by a large and appreciative congregation of hotel guests and Maltese from the surrounding area.

I must say that the present generation of the Macallef family who are now managing the 'Wavecrest' have inherited much of the vision and expertise of the founders. Providing good, wholesome entertainment for their guests is high on their list of priorities, and in that regard, the employment of two entertainment coordinators is an enlightened gesture, much appreciated by their visitors.

Don and Wendy are British, highly professional and popular with everyone. They make a wonderful partnership – Don, suave, sophisticated, elegant, and with a classy BBC speaking voice, Wendy, attractive, stylish, athletic, friendly and warm. Ballroom and sequence dancing is their speciality, performing it, teaching it, and boy, do they ooze class on the floor? They also organise and conduct walks, bingo, bridge, bowls, quizzes and a myriad of other interesting and entertaining pursuits. They are the life and soul of the hotel, and when they take a break, the atmosphere and ambience certainly drops down a few notches.

I must mention the excellent library provided by the hotel for the many avid readers among the guests. This is a much appreciated innovation, managed by Don, but ably assisted by bookworm, and man of many parts, Ben. Ben is amazing, a retired Yorkshire man, spends winter here, and is one the most popular characters in the hotel. He is a live-wire, involved in everything, and in the library, if a particular book is requested, Ben will locate it – if not, it doesn't exist.

I'm not a 'Disco Dancer' or a 'Rock-n-Roller,' and I have to confess, I'm no good at 'Sequence' or 'Ballroom Dancing' either. Believe me, it's a serious handicap in a place like the 'Wavecrest,' and I do feel unfairly deprived. But tonight in the ballroom, after a bit of a binge with this crazy gang, I am strongly tempted to take the floor and have a go at whatever the band strikes up. Luckily, for my self-respect, and the wellbeing of my potential partners, on mature reflection, I defer to my better judgement, stay where I am, and stick with the sauce.

It's just as well that I have a fellow traveller in Trevor. He is no 'Fred Astaire' either, and confines his time in the ballroom to a few pints, observing and making droll comments on the demeanour, the steps, and the inflated egos of the 'Strictly Come Dancing' fanatics gracing the floor. If it wasn't for Trevor's company, I'd be isolated and alone, because the other two members of the gang have no qualms about abandoning us for the lure of the dance floor.

Take Len for example. You'd think at his age he'd have enough dancing for one life. Oh no, he thrives on it, so much so, that I honestly believe it's the dancing at the 'Wavecrest' that brings him to Malta for three months every year. He's a proper little 'dancing master', never misses a dance – especially the Rock-n-Roll sessions – and at the end of the night, I've noticed some women trying to resist his repeated invitations – jaded out, when 'Lord of the Dance' would only be getting into overdrive.

I have to tell you a little story of an incident that occurred last year, hilarious for us, but devastating for Len, when he found himself in 'hot water' with the hotel management. He took a shine to a shapely elderly lady, mainly because of her dancing, particularly her 'Rock-n-Roll' dexterity – he felt a special synchronisation between them – repeatedly invited her out on the floor, and despite her protestations, would not accept no for an answer. The heavy beat of the rhythm and the thrill of the swing seemed to inject new energy and exuberance into Len's performance, and it was soon obvious that his partner was under severe pressure to keep up. To her credit, she didn't throw in the towel, and although appearing to be on the verge of a heart attack, she bravely battled on to the end.

Of course, our eighty-two-year-old rocker was exhilarated, boasting that it was his best ever night's dancing, and he couldn't wait for the following night. When I met him at breakfast the next morning, it was a very different story; he looked forlorn, stunned and depressed.

"What's the matter, Len? You look a bit rough."

"I've got a red card – suspended."

"Suspended! What do you mean? – Explain."

He revealed that the Entertainment Manager had informed him that he was suspended from dancing for seven days, due to a complaint received from a guest.

"What was the complaint?"

"Over exuberant dancing and harassment."

Although Len was deadly serious in relating the episode, I was about to explode in laughter, but somehow managed to suppress it. I knew that it was no more than a well-planned hoax, probably perpetrated jointly by Charlotte and the Entertainment Manager, with whom she had an extra friendly association. But, as they say, *all's well that ends well,* and later in the day, the suspension was lifted, and Len was back on the dance floor that night, friskier than ever.

That was a year ago. Tonight Charlotte hasn't got time for any similar little tricks. She seems to be preoccupied with a young whippersnapper at least half her age. From the moment he appeared, and snatched her away from us and our little binge, they have been inseparable, two besotted wraparounds, smooching on the dance floor, lost in a deep trance of love and emotion. That's the last we'll see of Charlotte tonight, but no doubt, we'll learn tomorrow how the night in 'Fairyland' unfolded, and the whole story of how it all ended.

I must admit that I do enjoy these little pranks and 'put downs,' as long as they are harmless to the victim, and accepted in the right spirit. Sure, why wouldn't I? Back in 'Paddy's-land,' where I come from, they are imbedded in our culture, part and parcel of everyday life, and I can assure you that you'd get precious little sympathy if you resented it, sulked, or tried to redress it.

I find the Maltese are a lot more reserved, take life more seriously, and would not be inclined to mock or poke fun at anyone, with the notable exception of bus drivers, the police, and the government. The British I meet here – especially retired men of the Defence Forces, and other well-heeled, articulate snobs – are not slow or backward in using the little vagaries of others for their own mirth and merriment, but they wouldn't be so accommodating if the boot was on the other foot – a flawed trait that over the decades in England, the 'Paddy's' experienced at first hand.

I've tasted a bit of it myself, here in Malta, but I have to say that 99.9 per cent of the British I meet are decent, friendly and respectful, and the couple of examples I'm going to mention are not from my reservoir of such incidents, but are 'once off's', and definitely exceptions to the rule. They were nasty little hiccups that occurred last year, both protagonists were British, my feathers were certainly ruffled, and to eliminate any suspicion of gender bias on my part, they were of opposite sexes.

Did you ever get the feeling that in trying to do something noble and good, you ended up making a right idiot of yourself. It happened to me, and even though I had the best of intentions and meant no harm, it backfired on me, and I can tell you, it wasn't pleasant. You know when you are on your own in a big hotel restaurant, bereft of company or conversation, you have plenty time to suss out the other diners – see who is coupled, in a group, or on their own. Now for me, being alone doesn't bother me one iota – I'm well contented with my own company, enjoying little silent chats to myself. But I do have sympathy for some – women especially – who appear to be lost souls that might welcome a friendly hello, or a little chat. One evening at dinner, a particular lady, well groomed and attractive, of similar vintage to myself, was sitting alone not far from my own table, and judging by her demeanour, and regular *'what ever brought me to this dive'* sighs, seemed to be the embodiment of boredom and isolation, prompting me to wonder if I could be of some little help. Having finished her meal ahead of me and about to pass my way, I decided to be the 'Good Samaritan' and offer some solace to cheer her up a bit and help her on her way. We made eye contact, I flashed my most benevolent smile, and performed my first stupid gaffe – I opened my big mouth.

"Excuse me, Madam, can I say hello? And perhaps….."

Well! She stopped dead in her tracks, straightened up, pierced me with a look that would turn milk sour, and exclaimed:

"Certainly not! How dare you interrupt me…I could report you to the management for harassment!"

Jerking her head defiantly back into the air, akin to a soldier on parade, she quick-marched out of the restaurant, leaving poor me stunned, humiliated and seething with some inner sensation that I couldn't identify. I felt sick, and for the first time ever, half of my dinner remained on my plate – the snobby bitch had turned my stomach.

The next morning, having recovered somewhat, I rose early as usual and went on my little walk. On returning, having used the lift, I was heading along the corridor of the eight floor to my room. A couple emerged from the adjoining room and were walking towards me. All was fine until the man spotted me inserting my key, and realised that I was his room neighbour from hell, and the culprit he wanted to attack. Swivelling on his heels, he yelled as he rushed back to me.

"Are you the bloke that kept us awake all last night?"

I was puzzled, and felt that he was either joking or mistaken.
"You must have been hearing things," I said with as friendly a smile as I could muster.
Well! Talk about a *'red rag to a bull'*, he mutated into a raging monster.
"You were pushing fucking chairs around all night – we never got a wink of fucking sleep, and I'm fucking reporting you to the hotel."
Now, I have been known to get my ire up if I'm subjected to some injustice or mistreatment, and I would let fire with all guns blazing if I felt I was in the right, when someone was accusing me in the wrong. This was clearly one such occasion, as the chairs he was referring to were no more than the little stool that fits under my desk, and which I may have slid in and out a couple of times before retiring to bed.
"You can report me if you wish – feel free – and when you've done that, there's a doctor's clinic over the street, where you can have your ears tested."
As he violently lunged forward to attack me, he was grabbed and restrained by his wife/partner, and as I turned the key in my door, I heard his parting shot:
"You're a poxy little Irish bollocks!!!"
"Wrong again," I replied, as I closed the door behind me.
Later, in pensive reflection, I tried to figure how it was, that the only two nasty incidents I experienced in all my years visiting Malta could happen in the same twenty-four hours, and I wondered what on earth I was being punished for. I decided to put it out of my mind – forget it – offer it up for my sins.

Now, over the years in Malta, I have been privileged to meet some wonderful people of all nationalities. One lady that I was blessed to know was from that idyllic part of England, Devon, and although it was a bizarre occurrence that led to our first acquaintance, it also sparked a warm friendship that has endured to this day. It was a scorching day, a few years ago, and along with hundreds of others, I was stretched out on a sun bed near the pool. Soaking in the hot sun, engrossed in a Hemingway classic, and oblivious to the comings and goings of the near-naked throng around me, I was startled when this elderly lady kicked my water bottle – which I had thoughtlessly left in her path – as she manoeuvred through the narrow gap between my stretched carcass and those of my near neighbours. It was an excellent kick – a real 'Frank Lampart' special – hilarious to me, but a mortifying incident for the kicker. I jumped up, followed and retrieved it, and found it none the worse for the penalty kick, more than can be said for the lady, who was highly embarrassed, profuse in her apologies, and offering to buy me a new bottle.

Of course, being the proper gentleman, I would have none of it, saying the whole incident was a thing of nothing and *could happen to a bishop*. Nonetheless, she arrived back shortly afterwards with a pristine new bottle of water, which I gratefully accepted, with an invitation to sit for a little rest while she fully regained her composure. She did, and we got on brilliantly. For at least an hour of non-stop chatting, Lily and I delved into our backgrounds, found lots of similarities, were totally comfortable and at ease in each other's company.

It was five years previously that she had lost the love of her life, her husband of forty years, her soul mate, her life, her all, and with no children, trying to cope alone without him proved a struggle that was almost beyond her. Advised by friends to take a little break in the sun, and on the suggestion of her travel agent, she decided to choose this little island. Just as it did to me, Malta cast its magic spell, captivating her, renewing her interest in life, raising her spirits, and it has become a 'home from home' for her ever since.
Now in her early eighties, healthy and happy, Lily spends nine months of the year in her quaint little bungalow in beautiful Devon, driving her car, pursuing her many labours of love: growing organic vegetables and flowers in her beloved garden, tending to her hives of honey bees, and three days a week working for the National Trust as a hostess in a big historic country house. I'm not surprised. She would be the perfect hostess for any promotion – tall, elegant, charming, friendly, warm, and with a heart of gold.

Her three months every year in Malta has gained her a multitude of friends. Usually to be found in the centre of some group or other, joining in the banter, telling jokes – some of them borderline – and spreading her charm everywhere, she is the life and soul of the hotel; an extra ray of sunshine to brighten our lives. She hasn't arrived this year yet, but no doubt we'll all be aware of her arrival. Her dazzling smile will light up the place, and her contagious, hearty laugh will reverberate throughout the hotel to signal her presence, cheering us all and enhancing our stay. For me, that penalty kick she took, scored a wonderful goal.

***

I'll finish this chapter by telling you a story that I was on two mind's whether I should or not. It is certainly relative to my Malta experience, but as it unfolds you will gather why I had reservations about an episode that gave me mixed memories, but also had a profound impact on me.

From the time I set foot on the Island of Malta, I have been singing its praises back home. None of my family had been spared my gloating, and of course, the whole object of the exercise was to encourage some of them to jump on a plane, and discover the delights of this little haven for themselves. It didn't happen – no one took the bait – until one day during my stay here in 2008, I got a call from my brother saying that he was coming for a week – I was delighted. Now, Simian was the one member of the clan that could well afford to go anywhere he wished – successful in business, his family reared, plenty spare time – as they say, *he wasn't short of a few bob.* His wife Marian usually went with him, but as they had a variety of holidays each year, this time she let him off on his own, released him into the 'safe custody' of his older brother, and trusted them both to be good boys.

His little Maltese odyssey of pleasure and exploration began as soon as he stepped off the plane. I had done a bit of homework, had a full seven day schedule ready, confident he would be up to it – I was determined to make it a week to remember, and vindicate all my bragging and boasting about Malta. We didn't hire a car, preferred to sit in taxi's and those little red mini-buses – less stress and strain, and more opportunity to savour the booze as well as the scenery – and over the course of the week we criss-crossed most of the island, and spent one whole day exploring Malta's beautiful little green sister, Gozo.

Simian was always a connoisseur of Chinese food, and during his stay he took me to a few strange restaurants for even stranger, multi-course dishes. I hadn't a clue what I was stuffing in, but it tasted delicious, and didn't have any after effects. I can't say the same for the beverage. Now, I suppose it's a bit unfair to blame the product when in fact, it's the abuse of it that does the harm. I don't like hangovers, and generally try to avoid them, but that week, I have to admit, a couple of the self-inflictions were rough enough, but they were worth the suffering, because in acquiring them we had great chats, crack and enjoyment, and the old liqueur played its part in egging us on. We had fun, food and drink in all the hot spots of the island – Valletta, Mdina, Sliema, St. Julians St. Paul's Bay, - returning back each evening to the Wavecrest for dinner, to be followed by another little session in Roy's bar. You can see it was hectic, and my little bit of forward planning was working like clockwork.

The day before his departure was Sunday, and I had arranged a particularly busy itinerary, having purchased a whole-day excursion ticket for a bargain price, and we certainly got great value for money. Up early, we were taken by coach to Valletta, and a visit to the famous 'Sunday Flea Market'. Squashed into a walled area beside the bus terminus, hundreds of stall holders were displaying and selling mountains of goods - food, clothing, jewellery, gadgets of all shapes and sizes – even including a large selection of cage birds and pet rabbits. Simian was fascinated and so absorbed in it all that I literally had to drag him away – our day was only starting.

Next stop was Sliema, and there we boarded a large boat for a harbour cruise. The Grand Harbour of Malta is world famous for its huge depth and massive expanse, brushing not only the shores of Valletta and Sliema, but also the three cities of Vittoriosa, Senglea and Cospicua, and it is also home to the huge world renown shipyards, and a range of important marinas, accommodating giant luxury yachts from many countries. The cruise took an hour, and we were treated to a light meal and unlimited quantities of surprisingly good wine, pumped from a tap like beer – a new one on me. It was marvellous to explore this world famous harbour from inside it, and having been taken to every little nook and crevice, we certainly saw it all, got some great photos, and had a most enjoyable experience.

Back on shore, we were whisked a few miles across the island for an afternoon's fun at the horse racing in Marsa. Now, as you know, I have been harping on, making comparisons between Malta and Ireland, and in general, blowing up Malta and running down my own old sod. Well, I have to tell you, the boot is on the other foot here. Horse racing in Ireland is truly world class and is internationally recognised as such. What we saw that day in Marsa was 'Micky Mouse' racing, and couldn't be spoken of in the same breath as Irish racing. I have found, and Simian did too, that if you are used to top class flat and jump racing, you just can't get your head around this trotting lark. But we were there to enjoy ourselves, and we made a valiant attempt to join the large crowd of obviously happy racegoers, studying the form, placing bets and cheering the finishes. Sadly, to our exasperation, neither of us managed to pick a winner out of ten races – says much for our judgement of trotters – but it was a unique experience and an insight to a type of horse racing that didn't grab us, but instead, added to our love and appreciation of our own little country's dominance in the 'Sport of Kings'

We were taken back to Bugibba, and, giving the 'Wavecrest' dinner a miss, we gorged ourselves on more mysterious grub in a posh 'Chinese' before hitting 'Murphy's Irish Pub' for a farewell session. Now, I better tell you here that Simian has dabbled in music all his life. An excellent guitar player, his 'Country and Western' group has for many years enjoyed popular acclaim throughout Ireland and even further afield. So you can see why, when he met Marty Rivers, the star entertainer of 'Murphy's' every weekend, they had a great little musical chat, to be continued later when the session was over.

The pub soon filled up with lots of Irish revellers, the music was great, and in the centre of it all were two brothers getting nicely inebriated, and regretting the fact that this was their last night together for a while. A little ***'Attention Please'*** from Marty hushed the crowd, allowing him to announce that they were privileged to have among them tonight a 'Country' singer from Ireland, and he was calling on Simian to come up and give them a few songs. Being at just about the right level of intoxication, he gladly obliged, and having donned Marty's guitar, preceded to strike up some rousing hits. The reception was mad – clapping, cheering, and calling for more Irish songs. Simian was in his element, and he soon had the whole pub singing with gusto such world renown Irish classics as 'Danny Boy', 'The Fields of Athenry', and 'Dublin in the Rare Old Times.'

It was a fitting climax to a memorable week for my brother and me, a week that I will cherish for the rest of my life. As he was bidding me farewell at the airport the next day, Simian promised to return soon again to savour more of Malta's delights, and I am convinced he really meant it. Sadly, he never made it back. That scourge of modern life, that evil invader, that thief in the night – cancer - came and took him – stole his young life – robbed the planet of a true gentleman of talent and integrity, and his family of a shining light with a gentle soul. Aged fifty-six and with many years of life ahead of him, he had to go and leave us all devastated, reminding me of the old Irish saying: *It's only the good die young.*

****

A Look Back

I was never a historian. My motto always was: let bygones be bygones; try and concentrate on today and tomorrow, and leave all that history stuff to the long-haired, bespectacled academics, who would reel off every little detail of the past, know nothing about the present, and even less about the future. But, in a place like Malta, that all goes out the window – you'd want to be a total zombie not to notice and appreciate the unique and incredible history of this little island and its people.

I have no intention of going back 5600 years to when the first Megalithic Temples were erected, but if I had, incredibly, they are still to be seen standing here, and are a great tourist attraction too. No, my fascination with Maltese history begins in 1565, because what happened then showed the world what the Maltese were made of, reminding all and sundry, that anyone taking these primitive, timid people for a 'soft touch' needed to think again, and it was the first real test of their spirit, tenacity and resilience. With their backs to the wall they displayed a reservoir of courage that would continue to manifest itself in many future invasions, unfairly perpetrated, but bravely repelled and defeated.

I suppose, the present-day cliché: l*ocation, location,* l*ocation,* could be aptly applied to Malta, and probably was the source of a lot of their troubles. Being stuck on the crossroads of the Mediterranean – a strategic spot in wartime – put them on the wish list of many greedy predators, and to hold their ground and their little country, they had to fight, defend, and defeat the bullies, and time after time they did this against all the odds, preserving their dignity, and their little island.

When the Knights of the Order of St. John were welcomed to Malta in 1530, it began 268 years of honourable rule by this Military and Hospitaller Order. They were the makings of Malta, and clear evidence of their inspiration, vision and resourcefulness can be seen today in the beautiful 'World Heritage' City of Valletta, the magnificent palaces, and the myriad of superb churches that adorn every corner of the island.

But in May 1565, the lookout soldier spotted the arrival of the dreaded Turkish armada. 40,000 troops landed on the island, convinced that they could set up shop with impunity, as Malta had only a meagre 8,000 fighting men. The Turks were in for a shock and a rude awakening. A fierce battle began, and for four blood-spilling months, the islanders stood their ground against massive bombardment in a heroic siege that remains legendary to this day. The attackers were sent packing, and the siege was lifted on 8th September, the feast of the birth of 'Our Lady', and the Maltese have always believed that their deliverance was mainly due to her Divine help.

The eighteenth century wasn't all sunshine for Malta either. With the French Revolution, the Knights lost most of their European influence, territory, and financial support, and as more elderly knights came to retire in Malta, their financial situation became critical.

In 1798, Napolean Bonaparte cast his greedy eyes on the little struggling island – a vital link between France and the Middle East for his planned Egyptian campaign. He used a mean little trick to try and hoodwink the Knights, and gain access to the island when, with his large fleet anchored off the coast, he asked for permission to enter the Grand Harbour to replenish the ships with water and other needs. He was only allowed to bring in four ships, and having taken that as an insult and a refusal, he forced his way in, took control, and settled down for a what he thought would be a long and fruitful stay.

Once again the Maltese mettle was tested, and they found themselves in yet another dog fight. With the help of the British, they managed to evict the French after two years of a fierce and bitter struggle. This put Britain in the driving seat, and in 1800, with the Knights weakened beyond recovery, they took over the administration of the island, staying until 21st September 1964, when they left and gave Malta back her independence. That date is proudly commemorated every year since, as is 13th December 1974, when Malta was declared a Republic.

Of course, no look back at Malta's history, however brief, would be complete without a mention of the two World Wars of the early twentieth century. In the first, (1914-1918) the Maltese were not directly involved in the terrible battles that killed millions. But they were still an important factor, providing aid and sustenance to the allied troops in need of medication and recuperation, after the various battles of the Eastern Mediterranean. They were nicknamed 'the Nurse of the Mediterranean' for the hospital services they provided.

The Second World War was to be totally different, and a much more tragic event for Malta, because only one day after war was declared on Britain and its allies, the island was attacked by Italy, under the Fascist dictator, Mussolini. Once again, the courage of the people was shown in spades, enduring daily bombardments from the air, repelling invasion attempts, and resisting the might of their attackers with nothing but flimsy land, sea, and air defences, and a spirit and determination to endure.

I was amazed to learn that Hitler's desire to invade and set up a base in Malta led him to drop more bombs on the island than on the City of London, and still those brave people resisted wave after wave of aggression from this evil monster. The women and children lived in underground shelters, while the men shouldered the burden of war, with little or no food for anyone, as convoy after convoy, bringing vital supplies from Britain were blown up on the way.

Miraculously, the island was saved and their second 'Great Siege' ended in 1943 when the Italian navy surrendered in the harbours of Malta. Amazingly, the date was 8th September, the same date as the ending of the 'Great Siege' of 1565, another certain sign for the Maltese of the Divine intervention of Our Lady, on the occasion of her birthday. In recognition of their courage and bravery during the war, Malta was awarded the George Cross by King George V1, a rare and unique distinction, cherished so much by the Maltese, that it is now proudly etched on their national flag.

For the past fifty years, Malta has developed and prospered. It is now an Independent Democratic Republic, a respected member of the United Nations, the Commonwealth, and the European Union. In recent years many important world figures have visited Malta. In 1989, American President, George Bush and Soviet Union leader, Mikhail Gorbachef met on the island, and in their talks, agreed to end the 'Cold War.' Pope John Paul and Pope Benedict have been here, and in 2005 the 'Commonwealth Conference' brought many dignitaries, including Britain's Queen Elizabeth.

So there you have it. My own little glimpse of Malta's past, a turbulent history, I'm sure you'll agree, that tested its people for their courage, dignity, spirit, perseverance, endurance and character, and in all categories, they were not founding wanting – they passed with flying colours.

****

You're Welcome, Sir.

It is my humble opinion that every person born has a uniqueness, a character, and a dignity that deserves recognition, appreciation, and respect. Throughout history, across the world, this basic tenet of civilisation has been denied and desecrated – a fatal flaw that has led to inequality, suppression, and disastrous conflicts and wars.

Malta has had its share of turmoil and trauma, but over long centuries of travails and tragedies, and to this day, they have managed to preserve the one great characteristic that sets them apart: charity and respect for each other, and courtesy, tolerance and friendliness towards all that visit them. That is what first attracted me to Malta, and, like a magnet, keeps pulling me back, because, as someone who regrets the abandonment of these high moral principles in his own country, to be the recipient of such affection and respect in a foreign country, is nothing short of inspirational, and I can't get enough of it.

"Good morning, Sir." "Good afternoon, Sir." "Good evening, Sir." "Thank you, Sir." "You're welcome, Sir." "Have a nice day, Sir." "Enjoy your holiday, Sir" Sure that's pure poetry! Sweet music to my ears. Where else would you get it? Perhaps in other places that I have yet to visit, but I would venture to suggest that nowhere would you find these greetings expressed with such goodwill, warmth and genuine sincerity, as on the little Island of Malta.

But the Maltese are not just all about being nice, courteous, and respectful. They also give tangible expression to these qualities by endeavouring to provide the best services and facilities their limited resources allow, for themselves and the millions of tourists they welcome every year. Take the Health Services for example. Now, for a little island, isolated in the heart of the Mediterranean, with less than half a million people, they have a 'top of the range' Health Service. How they provide it on such meagre resources baffles me. The Health Centres, Medical Clinics and Hospitals are second to none, and available free of charge to their permanent residents. But, as you'll have noted by now, I keep emphasising that the Maltese are in no way greedy, and they gladly share this wonderful facility with their visitors at a very reasonable cost.

I have been the beneficiary of Maltese health care on two occasions, and in both instances, I was pleasantly surprised with the efficiency, skill and genuine warmth of the professionals that treated me, and, coming from a country with a cash-devouring, malfunctioning monstrosity, that passes for a Health Service, it's no wonder I'm impressed.

The first health scare I had was a few years ago, and although it turned out to be trivial enough, my Maltese carers weren't taking any chances. For a few days after arriving, I had difficulty walking due to a pain in the calf of my left leg. I called to a private clinic near the hotel, and on examination, and being informed that it had been bothering me on the plane too, the doctor decided to send me to the hospital for scanning – he needed to have it checked for 'deep vein thrombosis.'

Within an hour, I was picked up by a taxi at the hotel, whisked off to St. James Hospital in Sliema – a new pristine private hospital – placed in a luxury day ward, and in a short time, I was in a treatment room surrounded by a maze of technology, with my left leg the whole centre of attention. While the *'results were being compiled and analysed,'* I was returned to my ward, where to my surprise, a lovely, hot four-course lunch was waiting for me. Now, that's what I'd call service.

I was then left to my own devices for a couple of hours, but that didn't bother me at all, I was bathed in such luxury and comfort – top of the range television, radio, and lots of reading material. I could have gladly stayed longer, but my consultant, an eminent specialist, trained in London, with a string of letters after his name, arrived with a folder – almost as thick as a telephone directory – containing every little detail of my scans, my diagnosis, my treatment, and having painstakingly explained it all to me in plain English, the result was: "No deep vein thrombosis, nothing serious to worry about, it was just muscular strain, and with a bit of physiotherapy, would be fine in a few days." It was. I still have the folder – a memento of the excellence of Maltese health care.

Last year I had occasion to call on this wonderful service again. One of my ears went 'on strike' – shut up shop – and to my utter consternation, a few days later the other one went blank. Now, being the *'leaving things on the long finger'* sod that I am, I suppose if I had to have a third one, I'd have carried on, but with my room neighbour politely telling me that he could clearly hear my television in his room, the penny dropped, and I decided to take action.

Now, the Mater Dei is a new 'state of the art' hospital, opened in 2007, and when I pass it on the bus to Valletta, I'm always wide-eyed and gaping, trying to comprehend this colossal sprawl of a building, wondering what it would be like on the inside. The two 'striking' ears now gave me that opportunity, and so at half past eight one morning, I turned up at the A&E.

As soon as I entered, the gigantic proportions of the building hit me – it's just massive, like a small town. 250,000 square metres, 850 beds, 25 operating theatres, 3,760 staff – no wonder it cost 600 million Euro to build. The efficiency and professionalism of the Maltese was evident everywhere. I was booked in, my personal, and my ailment details were computerised, and, armed with a comprehensive print-out, I was sent on a well sign-posted journey by 'Rolls Royce' lifts and 'street-long' corridors to the ENT department, that was akin to a space laboratory. There I was welcomed with a warm

handshake and a friendly smile by a tall, shapely specialist – no more than twenty-something – and ushered into her treatment room. She soon discovered why my ears went 'on strike' – years of wax build-up had formed an impregnable fortress in both, and it was a miracle that at some stage my head didn't go on fire. Many years ago, I did have my ears syringed by my local doctor, who injected hot water with a gun, and after a long and patient struggle, got rid of the wax and opened the ears. No guns in the Mater Dei. My wax-bursting expert used a selection of little electronic suction pumps, which were so powerful that I was beginning to wonder would she unwittingly suck out the few scarce fragments of my old brain too. The whole job only took her fifteen minutes, and towards the end I casually enquired:
"A lot of wax?"
"Enough to make two candles."
"Oh, that much! Feel free, I won't charge you for it."
She typified the endearing Maltese personality and sense of humour. In the space of one hour, I was on my way back to my hotel, and, although there isn't much of it in Malta, I could actually hear the grass growing.

***

I don't know if many people are affected in the same way – I suspect not – but I have a little medical problem that I may as well tell you about. It's to do with water – or more to the point – the control of it – or better still, the lack of control of it. Now, to begin, I want to ease your anxiety, and assure you that, on the best scientific advice available, I don't have 'prostate cancer' or 'diabetes' –

touch wood – I'm touching it now – my head – but I do have an acutely chronic condition: 'Piddle-itis' – a new medical term of my own invention – and it's akin to a pain in the neck, especially when I'm out walking. The symptoms are plain and simple – an intense urge to urinate every half mile – but its behaviour is most erratic – in the vicinity of plenty public toilets it loses the urge, but in an area bereft of such conveniences, it goes berserk, and will not relent without relief.
Now, I've done some research and have studied the progression and direction of the condition, and through a process of elimination have discovered a definite link to another condition: 'Caffeine-itis' another of my invented medical terms - a condition that coincidentally, I also suffer from. I hope I'm not losing you in all of this, but another weird discovery I've made regarding the two conditions is that the elimination of one, automatically eliminates the other. I tell you, it's crazy – I just can't go on – the burden of comprehension is too much for my little brain – I give up. Anyway, I'm bursting for a pee.

Now, all of that – actually true – is by way of an introduction to a subject that has exercised me for many years, not only in Ireland, but everywhere else I happen to be. Public Toilets. Ireland is a disaster area in the provision of public toilets. There are a few in the cities and large towns, but you'd want to be a long-standing resident to know where they are located, and if by some miracle you did happen to find one, it would probably be one of those French robots that locks its door automatically, and refuses point blank to open it unless you feed its greedy gob with 50 cent – an expensive pee, you'll have to agree. You could walk street after street all day in agony without finding one, and end up crouching into a restaurant loo, having been forced to buy an unwanted coffee, that you leave behind, as drinking it would only bring more agony. It's a disgrace and a scandal, and I make no apology for charging the buffoons responsible with gross neglect and dereliction of duty.

In the matter of public toilets, Malta to me, is a breath of fresh air, and an example to other more affluent countries, of how to properly treat their people. For a little country with limited resources, their generous provision of these essential conveniences – free of charge, clean and serviced daily – is a credit to their concern and respect for their own citizens, and those that visit their land. Take a bow, Malta, and a sincere 'Thank You' from this victim of 'Piddle-itis'

***

I can never get my head around this question, let alone answer it: How come the 'Maltese Bus' is so famous and revered, that it graces the mantelpieces of homes in all corners of the world? I know they are attractive to look at – but so are many other things – and I admit they are ancient, ornate and colourful, but is that a plausible reason for intelligent, well-travelled tourists to become so besotted with these little steel boxes on wheels, that they want to buy them, bring them home, and love, honour and cherish them for evermore. I find it astonishing, but it's true, and it has become too much of a mystery for my minuscule brain to unravel. It has also become a great money-spinner for the makers of these little model buses, and for the hundreds of souvenir shops that stock a myriad of them in all shapes and sizes, flog them like hot cakes, and in all of this, indirectly promote Maltese tourism throughout the world.

Of course, the big difference between the colourful imitations in the shops and the real thing, is that the little souvenirs are silent, harmless, and don't emit poisonous pollution, while the real live vehicle is the opposite in every respect. For ten years I've vibrated around Malta in those rickety tin boxes, my inside feeling like a cocktail being shaken, my body absorbing pneumonia-inducing drafts, and my lungs clogged with the passive smoking of lethal and obnoxious gases. The old pot-holed roads of the island carried thousands of these antiques for as long as most Maltese living today can remember, and while the passengers gracefully retired after their life's work, these old 'bangers' and their ageless drivers worked on to shake, rattle and roll a whole new generation.

The drivers were a law unto themselves. No age restriction existed, because most of these old veterans actually owned the buses, and were on self-employed contracts with the government. Their longevity, demeanour, and laid-back disposition, made a perfect match for the old vintage wrecks they were driving. They sauntered along at their own speed, oblivious to timetables, load restrictions, or pollution controls – nothing ever fazed them.

I'll tell you a little story that always gives me a chuckle whenever I recall or relate it, an incident that illustrates clearly the casual approach of these archaic operators, and would be really funny, were we not talking about the delivery of a vital public facility, and the only one available to the travelling people of Malta. I was returning from a day in the city of Valletta, and waiting at the bus terminus to board the 49 to Bugibba. Like the taxi-rank system, you took the one at the head of the queue, and your luck on the day determined the age and wellbeing of the antique you got – that day mine was down, so I eased myself into a true relic of old decency, driven by another survivor of history, and with a full load of perfectly contented, swaying passengers, we wound our way out of the city in the general direction of Bugibba.

It was mid afternoon, the atmosphere on board was casual and relaxed as we snaked along, all moving in harmony with the gentle shimmying of the old shaker. We made a few stops, said goodbye to a few and hello to a few others, in a time consuming interlude, as the addled old cashier struggled with the intricacies of "this newfangled money they sent us from Europe to replace our beloved Maltese Lira."

Almost at our destination, we made our penultimate stop, that would certainly have been our final stop, were it not for the ingenuity of our much-maligned driver, who held his nerve and resolved a tricky situation without fuss or bother. The big gear lever, standing tall in the front, refused to engage when requested, and seemed to have popped out of its slot below, just swinging around like a stick in a bucket of water. We were stuck – couldn't move an inch. Heads turned as we looked bewildered at each other, wondering how far we had left to travel, and how we would cope with an unexpected long trek on a hot afternoon. Without an explanation, an apology, or even a glance back in the direction of his passengers, our driver got out, went around to the rear boot, returned with a large toolbox, and preceded to unscrew the large steel plate that surrounded the gear lever. The removal of the plate left a big gaping hole in the floor, but also gave access to the gearbox.

Back in his seat, with the plate, gear lever and tools strewn over the floor, our driver/mechanic calmly, without a word, or even the slightest gaze in our direction, continued the journey, changing the gears with a large screwdriver and giving us the little added bonus of a bird's eye view of the road moving beneath us. Sure where else would you see it except on the little quaint and charming Island of Malta?

Alas, that's all *'water under the bridge' now.* At long last, the little old iconic yellow buses are no more – banished into oblivion – not at the behest of the Maltese or the government, but because of pressure from the EU, insisting that enough poisonous gas has been inhaled, demanding the retirement of the entire fleet of wrecks, the elderly owner/drivers be compensated, and the only derogation granted was the retention of the fleet of models on the shelves of the souvenir shops.

So, on the 1st July 2011, a new dawn awakened for the long suffering commuters of Malta. A Swedish company, Arriva, launched their brand new fleet of luxury buses, rescheduled the routes and timetables, and hiked the fares to previously unheard of levels. This complicated reorganisation caused massive upheaval for the travelling public, created chaos and confusion, and almost brought down the government.

The daily newspapers had pages of horror stories of people stranded and scorching at bus stops in isolated villages, commuters arriving hours late for work, and long cumbersome bendy buses causing havoc, trying and often failing, to negotiate sharp corners and narrow thoroughfares. A lot of these problems could have been avoided if enough preparation and forward planning had been done. Such a huge change - unwisely made at the peak of the tourist season – using a whole new team of inexperienced drivers, was bound to backfire and blow up into mayhem, widespread confusion, and frustration.

Following some serious reviewing and rescheduling under a new high powered committee, headed by no less than the prime minister, things are slowing improving. They will eventually get it right, and I've no doubt that the decision to give the job to Arriva, a reputable international bus company, operating successfully in many countries, was an inspired decision. It's just a pity they didn't get off on the right foot, but I suppose, coming from where they were, a smooth transition was too much to expect, and probably in a couple of years,

Malta will have an efficient, streamlined transport service, and all the travails of the past will be forgotten.

I must admit, I haven't, as yet, joined the queue to buy a little model yellow bus for my Irish mantelpiece - I just might now. It would be a nostalgic memory of a unique phenomenon – 'The Maltese Bus'

****

Here and There

I'm not sure if it's just me, but when I arrive in Malta for my winter hibernation, I seem to require at least two weeks to get myself in situ, to become acclimatised to my new surroundings, and not feel like 'a fish out of water.' It's probably mainly due to my age, or perhaps my old penchant for a highly structured existence, and a strict daily routine. Whatever it is, it's always a slow process easing myself into a suitable comfort zone, where things like stress, strain, and worry, are strictly excluded.

So, after two weeks of this psychological adjustment, I feel I'm now well and truly stitched into the fabric of Malta, and ready to resume normal existence. The litmus test of my mind's transition is when I begin to get a progressive urge to forsake the familiarity and protection of the hotel, and venture through the island to revisit old haunts, or explore new ones. Today, I'm responding to that feeling by heading to the bus terminus in down-town Bugibba to board the 31 for a day in my favourite city: Valletta.

In the days of the old yellow buses, you paid the driver 54 cent for a ticket that covered your fifteen mile, 'adventure trip' to the capital. Today, I have to master the workings of a computerised machine, feed it 2.60. Euro, on receipt of which, it spits out a full-day ticket, covering me for unlimited trips – a hundred bus rides if I feel inclined - only snag – they must be all taken today. Hold on now – there's something weird about this. It's crazy. I'm being flogged something that I don't need or want. Back to the machine I go for an explanation, which makes things even worse. I learn that on presentation of a Maltese Identity Card, my day ticket would cost only 1.50. Euro. So I pause, and try to get my head around this – put it all in a concise little nutshell. How can I have an Identity Card? – I'm not Maltese, or a permanent resident – so I pay 40% more because I'm a visitor – and from another EU country at that. I've now got the gist of it. To say I'm not impressed would be the under statement of the year.

Anyway, my anger subsides somewhat as we move off, and I sit back in what I have to concede is the sheer luxury of this new 'Arriva' bus, compared to the ramshackle bone-crushers that went before, and to further appease my sense of having been ripped off, the 'Times' on my lap tells me that the EU have begun an investigation into Malta's new bus fares, to determine whether they discriminate against visitors from other EU countries. Well, can you believe that? *'Wonders will never cease!'* But I won't hold my breath.

We glide along smoothly towards the village of Mosta, a busy little place, dominated by its wonderful centrepiece: 'The Mosta Dome.' The building of this gigantic church, with its world famous dome, was an incredible achievement for the parishioners. Looking at its astonishing height and massive overall dimensions, you wonder how they did it with the primitive construction equipment available in the nineteenth century – it's no wonder it took thirty years to build.

The location of the village near to the Ta' Qali airfield placed it right in the path of attacking planes during the Second World War. On one such raid in 1942, several bombs were dropped around the church, with one actually piercing the dome, landing on the floor, where three hundred people were attending Mass, and incredibly, it failed to explode. No one was injured, the dome was only slightly damaged, and to commemorate the miracle, the empty shell of the bomb can be seen today in the sacristy of the church.

On through the town of Naxxar, (pronounced Nashar – X = sh in Maltese) with its neat residential estates, rows of little snug dwellings, and inevitably, an impressive ornate church dominating the square. We pick up a few passengers, and roll on through the busy shopping town of Birkirkara to our next main stop: the huge sprawling edifice: the Mater Dei Hospital, where queues of people are waiting for various buses, a measure of the sheer volume of people connected to the hospital – workers, patients and visitors.

In through Msida, past the extensive Yacht Marina, which is packed to capacity with hundreds of expensive and luxury craft of all shapes and sizes, and I can't help thinking that some people have money in Malta, and plenty of it too. At the far end of the marina is the Armed Forces of Malta Naval Base, located in a little quiet corner known as Hays Wharf. Not much to see – a few small patrol vessels tied up beside a compound – but they perform important functions: fishing control, border patrol, and rescue services. Like most Maltese they take things easy when all is quiet and peaceful, but if you happen to be fishing illegally, importing drugs, or an alien, trying to sneak in, you'd soon bump into them, and I can assure you, the encounter wouldn't be funny.

Although every seat in the bus is now occupied, plus about thirty standing in the centre aisle, we persist in picking up more, and passing through Floriana, we are packed like sardines in a tin. Nobody seems to care, everyone is happy and contented as we reach our destination: The Valletta Bus Terminus.

For enduring decades of primitive travel on ramshackle, vintage buses to and from this major city, and having to suffer the indignity of a filthy unkempt dump for a terminus, the Maltese commuters deserve some kind of an award for their tolerance and forbearance. Year after year I have *'been there; done that',* and on each visit I have tried my best to close my eyes to the squalor, disorder and disarray, and wondered when the penny would drop, and the long-suffering travellers would get what they deserve: a clean, user-friendly Bus Terminus.

It was a sprawling expanse of utter chaos. Hundreds of the old relics on wheels arriving, departing, shunting, reversing, or just abandoned haphazardly, adding to the perpetual acute congestion. Hundreds of mesmerised passengers loading and unloading, at a myriad of unspecified points, crowds moving in all directions through the maze of mayhem, assembling at wrong locations, and an army of exasperated, blue-clad 'inspectors' of every age, shape and demeanour, trying desperately to guide them and ease the bedlam and confusion.

Around the perimeter, the old open-fronted shops did a roaring trade, but their old stalls and ancient kiosks gave a shantytown appearance, and they contributed much rubbish to the whole litter-strewn area. The massive concrete centrepiece: 'The Triton Fountain' gave some navigational guidance to stray travellers like myself, but even that seemed to have suffered from the decades of neglect and make-do – its once powerful team of water spurting jets, now tired and weary, like old men, could muster no more than a weak trickle.

Like the old buses, this is now thankfully, all in the past, and today I see a whole new order. A long line of designated terminals, clearly signed and numbered, wide open spaces, newly paved, spotlessly clean walk-ways, pristine new seated shelters and information desks, liberally located and manned by friendly staff. Lovely new buses arriving and departing on time, to and from their correct gates, and a new army of white-shirted officials efficiently, and with calmness and courtesy, advising, guiding, and ensuring the whole operation ticks over smoothly, without the slightest fuss or bother. What a transformation! I could hardly believe my eyes. The penny finally dropped!

Even 'The Triton Fountain' is earmarked for a two-million Euro reconstruction. The old pumps will be removed, and more powerful modern ones installed, and I can see the old jets rediscovering the verve and vigour of their youth in a display of sexual spurting to justify their two-million restoration. I look forward eagerly to seeing that, and all the other regeneration work completed, all of which will be a welcome boost, and a fitting 'City Bus Terminus,' after all those years of procrastination and neglect.

***

Each morning as I rise, I count my blessings, and thank the Lord for another new day in a life of health, wealth and happiness. The 'wealth' bit may be misleading, so I better explain. You see, my wealth is not measured in monetary terms, but in all the other great gifts that adorn all our lives, and that, regretfully, we often take for granted. One is the energy, inclination, and opportunity to travel the world, and see many wonderful places.

I have to tell you, that I'm not a great 'Big City' person – preferring the wide open spaces, green hills, sleepy valleys, and panoramas of lush green landscape. But while a few cities do captivate me, most of the world-famous ones certainly do not. I have walked the streets of many of these much heralded, iconic metropolises, and failed to get that awe-inspiring sensation that excites others. Perhaps it's just me, but with a few exceptions – Edinburgh, Amsterdam – there's a sameness about them all – sprawling, concrete jungles – that sends me home wondering what I missed, that the others saw.

Valletta, the capital city of Malta, is for me, the jewel in the crown of great cities, has enraptured me since the first day I entered through its magnificent gates, and continues to warm my heart with every step I take along its welcoming streets. Most cities around the world originate spontaneously, and evolve in a haphazard jigsaw of urban sprawl, with little or no distinguishing lines to indicate where the city ends and the country begins. Not so, Valletta. It becomes crystal clear as you enter, that here is a purpose built city, brilliantly designed in Baroque architecture, massively fortified, painstakingly embellished, and with an intangible charm and character built in, that I can't identify, but is there in spades.

When the Knights of St. John arrived in Malta in 1530, this area of the peninsula was uninhabited, except for a few farmers and fishermen, some small dwellings, and perhaps a little church. But these holy men had more upstairs than their faith in Divine Providence. This wonderful location, high up on a plateau, and looking down on one of the great harbours of the world, soon caught their eye, seeing it as the ideal site for a big walled and fortified city, and immediately began building it. The UNESCO World Heritage City that is Valletta today, is a glorious legacy of the Knights, and a testament to their wonderful vision and devotion to excellence.

It's not by any means a big city - in some other countries it would be classed a handy-sized town - but there's such logic gone into the planning of it, it strikes me that the Knights, like me, had a penchant for tidiness – *a place for everything and everything in its place.* I always wonder why other cities couldn't have designed a streetscape like this – a walker's dream – laid out in a grid-iron design, with three, 'straight as a gun barrel' main streets, slicing through from one end to the other, and a myriad of equally straight side streets intersecting the main ones, and all linking up at various points to form quaint little open squares, where down through the centuries, crowds have gathered for pageants, ceremonies, and important special occasions.

Valletta, being surrounded on three sides by deep water, is entered through its enormous gate at the Floriana end, a splendid double arch of Baroque elegance linking up with the great walls and fortifications that form an impregnable fortress ringing the entire city. These walls are gigantic in height and width, and having 'measured' them all the way round, I suspect that any intruder contemplating illegal entry, would need to have had some previous experience on Mount Everest. Beyond the city gate the entrance is quite narrow, and for a moment you get the feeling of being enclosed and restricted. Perhaps that's why Valletta's designers created a large empty area directly inside, and named it Freedom Square.

For all my ten years coming here, that's the way it was - this time it's all changed – it's now a bloody building site. Outside and inside the main gate, the fortifications at both sides, the square inside, the walls, everything is covered and hidden behind massive partitions, form-work and scaffolding, leaving just a narrow sheeted corridor for the masses to get through. What's it all about? Well, it's about the present day rulers of Malta, spending almost a hundred million Euro on a new face-lift for Valletta, giving it a shapely new mouth, sparkling new teeth in the form of swanky new parliament buildings, a new open-air Opera

Theatre, and a new embellished Freedom Square, still free, but only half its previous size.

I knew in advance of my visit that this work had started – courtesy of the Internet and the 'Times' – but it didn't prepare me for this enormous upheaval, and while I'm all for renewal and modernisation, I hope this 'world famous Italian architect', Renzo Piano – *how about that for a name* - who is entrusted with the design, will be up to the job, and following this risky face-lift, I will be able once again to recognise my old beloved Valletta.

Since 1974, Malta has been an Independent Democratic Republic, and the Maltese are so proud of that status and distinction, that the main street of their capital city is named Republic Street. What a clever way to let the world know, and no better way, because every time I walk this famous thoroughfare, I feel the whole world is here. They haven't come for the shops or the shopping, sure, the great international brand-names are all here, but compared to the massive arcades in most big cities, what is here would be classed as no more than little huckster shops. No, they are here to soak up the special ambience of a unique city, and Republic Street is its heartbeat, the assembly point of a great cosmopolitan togetherness, a sharing and appreciation of the delights of this ancient and ornate Capital.

It's only mid-morning, and already I'm in the presence of a moving mass of multinationals. I see all face shapes and skin colours, and it would take a better brain than mine to work out where they all came from, but they are here, and their presence enriches the atmosphere, and I'm sure also enriches the coffers of the Malta government's exchequer funds. But where are they all going? Well, some are just strolling along, browsing the shop windows on one side, and no doubt, will do the other side on their way back, but most are on their way to the many important landmarks that dominate this great street, particularly the Grand Master's Palace, the National Museum of Archaeology, and the world renown Cathedral of St. John.

Whatever about the others, it's to the Cathedral I'm heading now – for the umpteenth time, but I don't care, I can't get enough of it. I suspect it has the same effect on thousands of other visitors, because it's one of the biggest tourist attractions in Malta. Basically, it's a sixteenth-century building with a seventeenth and eighteenth-century interior. A famous Italian artist, named Mattia Preti, dropped into Malta in 1661, and preferring it to home, stayed there. It was a stroke of luck for Malta, because his genius is etched all over Valletta, none more so than the interior of this great cathedral.

The place is crowded, silence is strictly enforced, and you flash a camera at your peril. Visitors gaze in awe at the majestic high alter, and the splendour of Mr Preti's work. The nave is said by those who know and understand these things, to be his masterpiece. The church floor is no less magnificent. Covered with 400 multicoloured marble tombstones, it is the last resting place of the famous Knights that conceived and created this great city, and also this iconic cathedral, and if I could read their language, I would know their names, and when they died – it's engraved on each tombstone. Of course, like all great institutions, there was a hierarchy. The top Knights were called Grand Masters – they were the bosses – and throughout the cathedral they are commemorated in sculptures, paintings and monuments.

You wouldn't want to be in a hurry when you visit St. John's Cathedral. To linger and absorb the artistic beauty of the myriad of side altars alone would take hours, but for me, the 'Wow' sensation is in the Oratory. Now, in the world of famous artists, the name 'Caravaggio' is legendary. He may have been a rogue and a blackguard, shunting back and forth between Italy and Malta – depending on which police force was chasing him – but his works have for centuries been priceless treasures, revered the world over. The most famous of them all is 'The Beheading of St. John', the greatest masterpiece of its time, and here it is, in all its explicit gruesome detail, looking down at me, sending my mind into hypnosis and my legs into jelly-sticks.

I always keep that intoxicating sensation to the end of my visit, because even among all the other great treasures here, nothing can follow that, and I make my exit and head for the nearest café for the uplifting sustenance of a strong caffeine-laced espresso.

***

Now, here is a question for you. Where would you go if you were looking for the best cup of coffee in Valletta – the home of hundreds of top class cafés and restaurants? Well, with that abundance of choice you would probably say the question was impossible to answer correctly. Not so – just follow me. I have escaped from the arresting spiritualism of

St. John's Cathedral, and into the swirling throng of Republic Street. I turn right, and there in front of my nose is the answer to the question: 'Caffe Cordina'

If this is regarded as the most famous café, not only in Malta, but internationally, if they have brewed the best coffee in the land for 175 years, if the visiting celebrities and dignitaries from around the world refuse to leave Malta without a cuppa in this coffee-shrine, then I say to myself: who am I to disagree? The people in here must be doing something right.

When Cesare Cordina was about to set up his café in 1837, he had two ambitions: to place it in the very best location in Valletta, and to provide the highest standard of food, service and ambience in all of Malta. He not only achieved both ambitions, but did it with style, establishing a rendezvous with a unique atmosphere of true Maltese charm and elegance, in the heart of his beloved city.

The location was an inspired choice. 244-245 Republic Street, it is surrounded by iconic landmarks – The Grand Master's Palace, the home of the Grand Masters for 200 years, now the Office of the President, and the Seat of Parliament, the impressive Bibliotheca, where scholars from all over the world come to study the massive book collection, and research the history of the Order, the magnificent Manoel Theatre, restored in all its splendour, with its beautiful gilded ceiling and tiered boxes, and just across the street, the stunning St. John's Cathedral. *Location, location, location.* Yes indeed, Mr Cordina was certainly ahead of his time.

Even the chosen premises was special in many ways. It certainly has had a long and interesting history. Built by the Knights in 1744, a large imposing building, they occupied it until the early days of British rule, when it held various public offices, after which it became 'The Grand Hotel.' But its central location caused it to suffer heavy damage in World War Two during the awful blitz that hit Valletta in 1942. Undaunted, Mr Cordina, not only restored it to its former prestige, but added beauty and character, making it the jewel of Maltese cafes.

I have to tell you that every time I enter, what I would describe as this ornate palace, I'm astounded by the exquisite grandeur of its décor. The magnificent vaulted ceilings are embellished with many wonderful works by Malta's most famous nineteenth-century artist, Giuseppi Cali. These unique paintings symbolise the previous rulers of Malta, and the diverse eras of the country's history. Other outstanding mural paintings depict the eras of the Romans, the Knights, the British, and more recent additions commemorate landmark dates – Independence Day, the birth of the Republic, and the joining of the European Union. Now, I ask, where else in the world would you find all that inside one coffee shop?

To-day, sadly, Mr Cordina is no longer with us, but his glorious legacy lives on under the guidance of his family. 'Caffe Cordina' still maintains the same high standard of quality and service that Cesare Cordina dedicated his life to, and in the same atmosphere of style, elegance and charm.

Now, where would you head for if you were in Valletta, famished, and dying for the best cup of coffee?

***

I must say one thing without the slightest fear of contradiction, the Maltese love their churches. Every little village has its own revered 'Basilica' with the dome dominating the skyline, and here in the capital, apart from the gem of them all, Valletta is blessed with many other, less celebrated shrines of worship, each so stunningly beautiful, that any one of them would be a worthy centrepiece in most cities and towns.

Speaking for myself, I have to admit that although I may not be enamoured by big cities, I just can't resist the temptation to visit churches. I don't really know why. It's certainly not a symptom of any great religious fervour, or a sneaky way of courting favour with the man above, it's just that I love the strange sense of spiritualism that hits me when I enter, the peace and solitude, and the feeling of escapism from this noisy bustling world to an oasis of pensive reflection, that, for a few moments at least, revives the soul, and keeps the old mind focused on the real meaning and purpose of life.

There are three parishes in Valletta and each have a beautiful church, with their own special dedication: 'Our Lady of Safe Haven', 'St. Agustine's Church', and 'The Church of St. Paul Shipwrecked'. The last named is particularly unique and beautiful, with many artistic treasures. The canvases, especially the main altarpiece, are magnificent, and the processional statue, by the world renown seventeenth-century Maltese sculptor, Melchiorre Gafa, is regarded as the best in all of Malta. On the 10th February each year – the feast of St. Paul's Shipwreck – this church is bedecked in all its finery and treasures, is the centre of devotion to the patron saint, and it is so sacred and important to the Maltese, that the day is always a national public holiday. No wonder they continue to thrive and prosper – with all that piety and religion.

I have now wandered up to the highest point of the city and I'm enjoying one of the greatest harbour views in all the world. High up on the bastions, this wonderful vantage point is The Upper Barrakka Gardens, a place so full of beauty, wonder, and visual adventure, that I can never leave Valletta without experiencing its magic, and I know the same applies to thousands of other tourists, because it is always crowded with equally enthusiastic sightseers.

Situated at the highest level of the fortifications facing the Grand Harbour, its view sweeps over, not only the harbour, but the rest of Valletta, as well as the great urban sprawl that is Floriana. Directly in front, I can see the massive fortifications of Fort St. Angelo, and the three cities – jutting out like long tongues into the harbour – with the exotic names: Vittoriosa, Senglea and Cospicua. I have walked every street of these mysterious 'cities' and I can tell you, they always give me a weird feeling that I'm taking a step back in time, and a stroll through ancient history. Also straight in front of me is the massive shipyards, with their huge dry-docks and gigantic cranes, reminding me that Malta is much more than historic monuments and Baroque architecture. They have important heavy industry too, and these internationally recognised shipyards are a prime example.

Looking down beneath my balcony, I can see a saluting battery of three large nineteenth-century guns, restored and ready to fire. Every day, at the stroke of twelve, uniformed members of a heritage society ceremoniously fire the guns, and if you happen to be close by, and unaware of it, the explosion and shattering bang would frighten the daylights out of you, and your underwear would do well to stay clean and dry.

Apart from the wonderful view, this garden has some notable monuments and works of art. It's the last resting place of British Governor Maitland, there's a monument to Lord Strickland, one of Malta's first Prime Ministers, another to the nineteenth-century world famous artist, Guiseppe Cali, whose work adorns 'Caffe Cordina,' and even the brave Winston Churchill is here in all his glory, looking relaxed and contented, and no doubt, enjoying the view.

So, after all that, I stroll back into the centre of the garden, find a table beside the little open-air café bar, order a cappuccino, and relax with a lovely feeling of wellbeing and contentment.

***

Refreshed and raring to go again, I skip out of the heavenly relaxation of the 'Upper Barrakka Gardens,' and head for another enchanting feature of the Grand Harbour: 'The

Valetta Cruise Port,' or better known now as 'The Waterfront.' But on my way down, I can't resist the urge to stop and linger for a while to admire once again my favourite building in Valletta. Of course, this richly endowed city has a feast of wonderful architecture, and choosing your number one building is certainly not an exact science, but to me, this one is special, and to be honest – not being an expert in the field – I can't really say why.

Perhaps, it's the wonderful 'Baroque' façade, with its intricate and unique ornamentation, or maybe it's the setting, high up on an elevated plateau, giving it a majestic dominance over the harbour and the surrounding areas. Whatever it is that brings this sparkle to my eyes, has the same effect on thousands of other tourists, because it is by far the most photographed building in Valletta. I'm telling you about 'The Auberge of Castile,' an eighteenth-century palace, designed by Andrea Belli, and in addition to its aesthetic beauty, it has a past history and a present prestige to set it apart, prompting curious trespassers like myself to gaze at it in awe, and snap it from every angle.

When the Knights of St. John set up in Malta, they organised themselves into eight different 'Languages' to represent the various parts of Europe from which they came. Each 'Language' had its own hostel, or 'Auberge' as they are known in Malta. Of the eight 'Auberges' built in Valletta, only five have survived. This magnificent building, that now fills my eyes with beauty, and my mind with admiration, is one of them, and to me, is the jewel in the crown.

I really can't drag myself away from this wonderful work of architectural art, and although I know I can't, I would love to shake the hand that steered the pen, that designed this masterpiece – Andrea Belli must have been a genius! No wonder the government of Malta commandeered this gem, completely restored and refurbished it, and made it the official 'Office of the Prime Minister.' The red and white Maltese flag, with its unique 'George Cross' flutters proudly and high above this hugely symbolic palace, and I'm sure that the Statesmen and World Leaders that frequent this 'Seat of Government' are, like me, impressed and astonished by its beauty.

Lawrence Gonzi, the Prime Minister, is certainly blessed, not only to be the leader of this great little country – prosperous and highly respected throughout the world – but also, to be the occupier of this architectural heaven.

***

So, I reluctantly turn away from my 'dream home' and freewheel downhill to water level and The Valletta Cruise Port. The descent from street level is so steep that the road takes a scenic zigzag route, easing the sharp decline, but adding a bit extra to the journey. I take the short cut, leaving the road halfway down, negotiating a couple of hundred steps, and rejoining the road below. I used to come up that way too until I discovered – by the thumping inside my chest – that it was probably too much of a 'heart stress test,' and the last thing I wanted to do was to die climbing the steps to my favourite city. Perhaps that consideration also crossed the mind of whoever decided to locate a small hospital on a clearing, halfway up the steps – an unusual site for a hospital, but apparently much used, and would certainly be handy in an emergency.

Speaking of steps, I must tell you of an experience I had a few years ago. It has absolutely nothing to do with Malta, but every time I encounter a lot of steps it comes back to me. I was in Rome for a weekend, and spent most of it exploring the Vatican. A notice board told me I could go up to the top of the dome of St. Peter's Basilica for the modest sum of seven Euro. Well, I thought; why not? A chance of a lifetime! I joined the inevitable queue, and when purchasing the tickets, we were told that a lift would take us up halfway, and we would climb the other half by steps.

The journey by lift was fine, whisking us up to a landing where we all assembled to continue our adventure. I have to tell you, I wasn't prepared for the rest of the climb – 350 concrete steps winding in a spiral barely the width of my shoulders, and nowhere to either pause for rest, or catch my breath. It was pure torture, and at times I felt like 'throwing in the towel' but with climbers in front and behind, I just couldn't stop. Perhaps it was meant to be a punishment for wretched sinners like me, or some stealth trick to enforce prayer – I don't know – but I can swear that when I had struggled to the top – with the old ticker pounding like a sledgehammer, and the lungs gasping for air – I prayed fervently in thanksgiving for my deliverance – what a ghastly place to snuff it. When I recovered and could enjoy the wonderful panoramic view of the 'Eternal City' from that celestial vantage point, I was glad I survived the torture.

Now if you are one of those multi-taskers that can perform incredible feats like reading a book while eating a meal – you know, one eye on the page and the other on the plate – and if you happen to be at it right now, I would gently suggest that you close the book and finish your meal. I know it's a strange request, and far be it from me to tell someone to stop reading my book, it's just a little forewarning that the next subject I'm going to talk about is 'horseshit' and it just might not be your favourite delicacy.

You see, every time I visit 'The Waterfront' in Valletta, as I'm strolling along the approach road, I have to pass by a string of horse-drawn carriages, parked, ready and waiting for business. Fine! They add to the atmosphere and character of the place, but of course, they add something else too, a carpet covering of green porridge, that spreads along the road, polluting the air with a pungent gas that overpowers every other aroma.

Now, don't get me wrong, I like the smell of horseshit – especially fresh out of the tube – and coming from Ireland, sure wasn't I reared on it, and bullshit too – but this Maltese stuff is different, smells stronger, lasts longer, and appears to be a blend of perfumes, that lingers on your person long after you've left it behind. I have given this a bit of thought, and I ask myself: is this meant to be part of the welcome for the millions of foreign tourists that daily step off big cruise liners and smell Malta for the first time? Do the powers that be want to solve the problem, or have they tried and failed? I think I may be able to help with a few options.

They could of course, wash the road every day – too costly? They could enact a bye-law – similar to the one for the dogs – enforcing the owners to pick up the droppings as they fall – not feasible? They could get rid of the bloody stinkers altogether – not possible? Well then, there is only one answer: put nappies on the horses! Oh, it's not nearly as funny or far-fetched as it sounds. They did it last year at the 'Lakes of Killarney' – Ireland's world famous beauty spot – but only after decades of warfare between the Jarveymen and the local council. In the end the council won, and now both the Jarveymen and the horses have got used to the nappies, and the roads that wind around those idyllic lakes and mountains are pristine clean and smelling of roses.

I'm sure it would work here in Malta too, but the extreme heat in summer might require a little tweaking of the nappy design. I'm thinking of perhaps a kind of arse-bib attached to the horses belly, extended around the hips and hooked to the front of the carriage. The only problem with that is the build-up of fresh horseshit right under the noses of the passengers, so as an alternative I suggest fitting a tank underneath the carriage, with a chute leading directly from the outlet, via the bib, to the tank. It would be a kind of under-carriage loo, and would hold a day's supply. I hope now that this is not all too technical or smelly for you – I'm only trying to be helpful.

Anyway, it's really not my problem, and if I still get the whiff of this old familiar aroma on my future visits, it won't stop me from filling my nostrils with it, on my way to The Waterfront.

I'm now in the heart of the Valletta Cruise Port, and I must say that it's as impressive to-day as the first time I came here, and sampled its unique atmosphere and old world charm. It certainly was an inspired decision to develop this old 'Pinto Wharf' on the northern shore of the Grand Harbour into what it is to-day: an ultra-modern cruise port, accommodating thousands of tourists disembarking every week from some of the world's greatest cruise liners. It stretches about one kilometre, and the centuries old warehouses and workshops lining the shore have been transformed, and elegantly refurbished into top class restaurants, cafes and shops.

To-day a massive Italian liner occupies the full length of the dock, towering above and dominating everything else. Three thousand passengers have disembarked, and are now sprinkled all over the immediate area. Some are on walking tours of the city, some have gone on luxury coaches to outlying places of interest, and some are happy to wander around here, sampling the Maltese cuisine, or browsing the wonderful array of shops, no doubt purchasing some unique Maltese glass and handmade crafts.

Tourism is the life blood of Malta, and in 2011, they welcomed over two million visitors. That works out at five tourists for every one Maltese citizen, and I feel certain that no other destination country in the world can match that. The cruise port has contributed hugely to those remarkable figures. This is its tenth anniversary, and each year its figures have increased. Last year 550,000 cruised in, and this year they welcomed 565,000. That's real money in any language, and I can see nothing but further expansion in this lucrative trade for the shrewd Maltese, and all I can say is: the very best of luck to them.

This wonderful development, 'The Waterfront,' has already won international awards for conservation of the architectural heritage, and is also becoming a popular venue for arts and music events. It is now the main venue for the famous Malta Jazz Festival in July, and an important 'Wine Fair' in August. Isn't it amazing how, with a bit of joined-up thinking and bold initiative, an ancient old wharf, that served the Grand Harbour for centuries, could be given this new lease of life, serving the wealthy travellers of the world, and at the same time boosting substantially, this little country's finances. Well done, Malta!

***

Valletta is such a vast treasure-chest of awe-inspiring places to see, that I could easily spend a week here, wear out a pair of boots, blister my feet, and still not have seen it all. It's mid-afternoon now, I feel happy enough with my rambling today, and being the lazy sod that never believes in self-inflicting unnecessary fatigue or weariness, I'm going to settle for today's little appetiser, and promise myself to return soon for a more extensive feast of this delightful city.

The strange thing about it is that I've done it all so many times before, but Valletta has some weird magnetic pull on me - and I suspect on many others too – that no matter how many times I have sampled these unique attractions, I'm lured back for more of that special mind-soothing tranquillity, that rare feeling of admiration and appreciation, hard to find elsewhere, but here in abundance, and I for one, never tire of it.

Now, in case this little book runs out of pages before I get a chance to return, I'm going to flash through some of the other Valletta highlights that I've discovered on past visits, and can't wait to see again, just in case you may be thinking of coming, and under the false illusion that spending one day in this gorgeous city will satisfy your appetite for pleasure – not a chance! Be prepared for the contagious condition called 'Valletta-Addiction Syndrome,' and be ready for a long trek over a number of days, complete with a good strong pair of boots, a robust wide-angled camera, clear eyes and an uncluttered mind, capable of absorbing a multitude of ambience, enchantment and glorious history. Don't say I didn't warn you.

The Casa Rocca Piccola, in Republic Street, is a sixteenth-century palazzo, built by Italian Knight, Pietro La Rocca, and is still the home of his descendent the 9th Marquis de Piro, himself a modern-day Knight. The many rooms in this palace are truly exquisite, and even more charming is the rich collection of antique furniture, silver and paintings, and the rare, historic costume museum. I find this a gem of a place to visit because it gives a fascinating insight into the customs and lifestyles of the Maltese nobility over 400 years.

Fort St. Elmo has history seeping through its ancient walls. Standing proudly at the southern end of Valletta, it harbours all the dark secrets of Malta's turbulent past. A guided tour of this eerie old fort relates the epic saga of the Great Siege of 1565, that heroic chapter in Malta's profile of courage, and also shows the grim former barracks where parts of the 1978 movie 'Midnight Express' were filmed. Each time I visit this old historic symbol, I'm whisked back through the centuries of Malta's glorious triumphs, aghast with amazement, and filled with respect and admiration..

'The National Museum of Fine Arts' – *now there's a grand title* – it's no less than it deserves, because as museums go, this one can compete with any in the world. Now, first of all, I must mention the building, because many people – far more qualified than me – regard this as the most beautiful and prestigious building in Valletta. To my uneducated eye, it isn't. I'm happy to give it number two, after the 'Auberge of Castile' *and that's my final answer*. But I will concede on one point: the main staircase in this wonderful palace is the most beautiful stairway in all of Malta. You won't be surprised by this coincidence: both houses were designed by the same man – our genius friend, Andrea Belli. Another old Irish saying pops up: *"The cream will always rise to the top."*

But of course, 'The Museum of Fine Arts' is all about the wonderful collection of paintings and sculptures within its walls, treasures truly mesmerising and priceless. All the great paintings dating from the fourteenth century are there, and by all the iconic artists too. Mattia Preti, of St. John's Cathedral fame, Matthias Stomer, Antonio de Favray, and the Maltese masters, Francesco Zahra, Stefano Erardi, and Giuseppe Cali. One of the highlights for me is the magnificent nineteenth-century Turner watercolour of the Grand Harbour – it just blows me away! Antonio

Sciortino's sculptures are well represented too – his work can also be admired in the various monuments dotted around the streets and squares of Valletta and Floriana, another genius in a land overflowing with them.

In addition to all these riches, I can also feast my eyes on an intriguing collection of artifacts and fine silverware, including medical equipment used by the Knights in their hospitals. I can never be in a hurry when I drop in to this heavenly oasis, and for someone so addicted to pleasure, this is one place where I'm in my element.

I think I've given you enough of a starter now to whet your appetite for a full feast of this remarkable city. Sir Walter Scott said, *"Valletta is a city built by gentlemen for gentlemen."* The gents he was referring to were of course, the Knights, and when you think about it, he was only partly right. Yes, it was conceived and created by the Knights, they named it after its founder, the Grand Master, Jean Parisot de La Vallette, and while they ruled Malta, I'm sure they were proud of their creation, but this honey-coloured, beguiling city has also served the Maltese, and enchanted the world for the past 430 years. I'll rephrase Sir Walter: *"Valletta was built by gentlemen to serve Malta and delight the world."*

****

Cats, Snails and Prickly Pears.

Here's another little question for you. What have cats, snails, and prickly pears got in common?
You don't know? I thought you wouldn't, because I myself have only discovered the answer recently.
All three are very dear to the hearts of the Maltese.

Now, before I ever set foot on this little island, if I had been posed the question: what do you know about Malta? Of course, being the honest joker that I am, I'd have to say in typical Irish impish guff: "Sweet feck-all!" But that's not entirely true, because for as long as I can remember, for some unknown reason, whenever the word Malta was mentioned, three things flashed into my mind: the Order of Malta, the Maltese Bus, and the Maltese cat. Why? Simply because they were famous around the world.

I have ranted on enough about the first two, so I must now pay homage to the little furry 'dotes' that for centuries have roamed the undergrowth of Malta's countryside, and nestled in the hearts of its people. Firstly, I want to lay my cards on the table and say that I have nothing but admiration for the Order of Malta, and I've always been fascinated by the Maltese Bus, but cats – even the world famous Maltese ones – have never endeared themselves to me. I have a huge prejudice against them – probably unfair – and dismiss everything positive about them, because I can't bring myself to forgive them for their ability to create the most foul odour the world has ever known: cat's pee. Now, please don't accuse me of racial bias, Irish cats have the same obnoxious powers, but of course, if it can be proven to me - after some infallible scientific experiment - that the Maltese cat's urine is more nose-friendly, I'll gladly revise my opinion, and take appropriate retribution. I have my doubts.

No, as cats go, to me they are all the same, but I will concede that the ones I've seen here are, for the most part, a pretty good-looking lot, and certainly a credit to the dedication and nurturing they receive from the Maltese 'cat-mothers.' Last year I happened to be returning to my hotel after a little stroll early one evening, and as I rounded a corner where on one side was a bit of greenery – a grassy area with some shrubs and low bushes – I was confronted with an entertaining performance, as good as any little theatre production that you'd pay money to see. Mammy-cat, surrounded by her baby-cats were having a little party, and it was a delight to behold.

I worked it out that it was dinnertime for cats, and all the locals were present and correct. The elderly lady was hosting the banquet, and twenty guests – I counted them – of all shapes, sizes, colours and demeanours, were tucking into scrumptious grub, so delectable, I almost felt peckish myself. Her little Ford Fiesta was parked by the kerbside, with the boot open, from which she magically extracted tin after tin of 'Kitty Kat', 'Paws', 'Whiskers' and various packets of other delicious delicacies, piling it on to twenty plastic plates, that she had already laid out. It was akin to the 'Miracle of the Loaves and Fishes,' the only thing she neglected to provide was serviettes, and I could see by the snouts and whiskers of some of the more gluttonous ones, that they could have done with them.

The cats, well, I'm no expert in feline study, but they appeared to be a mixture of cross-breeds and hybrids, with a variety of colours and characteristics. Some were fat and cuddly, others were long and skinny, some had a friendly, placid demeanour, but a few had that wild, threatening stare that I blame for giving 'cat's eyes' a bad name.

The cat-mother was so absorbed in her 'waiting and serving' that she didn't notice the nosy Irishman watching her every move, so in response to my little cough, she turned, smiled, and I was able to deduce that she was neither loony, demented, or otherwise retarded, just a kind old lady dedicated to the care and welfare of her feline family of appreciative babies. I gingerly took a few steps forward and ventured a little chat with her, which she kindly engaged in, but without eye contact as she was too busy, and anyway, I was only an extra in this little theatrical scene. I'm glad I did, because I soon realised that I was conversing with, not only a devout feline missionary, but an authority on the cat culture of Malta, reeling off statistics, procedures, and matters of policy ad lib - a mind-boggling fund of knowledge that surprised and impressed me greatly.

I learned that Malta has hundreds of thousands of cats living wild, and being cared for by a myriad of charities, and regulated by several prominent animal welfare organisations such as 'Happy Paws,' (*what a name*) 'Noah's Ark,' and

'Island Sanctuary.' The country is also saturated with 'Charity Shops' run by teams of dedicated women – most of them retired British, permanently resident in Malta – and evidence of the generosity they receive is reflected in the booming trade they generate. This fundraising, together with donations and legacies, is what keeps the cats fed, but now they have embarked on an even more expensive money-eating project: the neutering of all stray cats. Bloody spoilsports - no more fun for the poor cats. One statistic my cat-mother friend imparted to me just knocked me off balance. I couldn't believe it – and I bet you will find it incredible too – that one unneutered female cat could be the source of 420,000 cats over seven years. That is some cat-sex! No wonder they have to 'nip it in the bud.'

It was time to leave my learned cat-professor, but before I did, I committed one of those stupid bloomers that over the years has cost me money and dignity. Casually, I asked: "How do *you* finance the purchase of all this cat food?" She straightened up with a sudden jerk, dived towards the car boot, retrieved a large round collection box, thrust it in front of me, with a pleading expression that said: "You will be generous Sir, won't you." After a frantic search of every pocket had only yielded thirty cent, I reluctantly and painfully had to revert to the wallet. Opening my big mouth cost me a lovely ten Euro note – of my scarce resources – and although I am now an expert on Maltese cats, I would never have dreamt that I would end up one of the largest cat benefactors in all of Malta.

***

The Old Emerald Isle where I come from has, like most other places, its faults and failings, but it still has some magical influence on the millions that had to leave it over the centuries. Some kind of magnetic force that grips their hearts, and will not let go until they return, like John F Kennedy, to the *"Green and Misty Isle,"* to the little dot on the map that spawned, and sent forth 'Poets, Presidents and Preachers' to all corners of the world. A favourite expression of the homesick Irish emigrants throughout the world is: "Some day I'll return to the Old Sod" and when you hear it you wonder how an old sod – that they hardly noticed before they left – could now generate such nostalgia and affection.

Well, of course, we 'Paddy's know the answer. No matter where we travel in the world, we never find a sod of clay so brown, so deep, so rich, or so fertile, than the lush carpet that envelops Ireland, and that's why we can feed the world and her children with our tender meat, our golden grain, and our succulent dairy products. And when we die, we are happy and contented to be gently laid into its loving breast, to snuggle and slumber in its bosom of solace and tranquillity

What, you may well ask, has all that got to do with Malta? A good question – Well, I'm about to explain, and you'll then get my gist! I, and thousands of other Irish gardeners spend our springs and summers cultivating that lovely rich sod, and it generously feeds us with an abundance of fresh fruit and vegetables, that keeps the smile in our eyes, and the healthy colour in our complexions. Of course, we have to be on our guard against thieving burglars: birds –

especially pigeons – rabbits, hares, etc. but by far the biggest enemies, and the most detested tyrants of them all are the snails, or slugs, that sneak in during the night – like an army of enemy tanks – obliterate all before them, and disappear by morning, leaving only their slimy trail of destruction, and the certainty that they would be back for more fun and feasting. No wonder the little evil monsters are the sworn enemy of the Irish gardener, and at every sighting are gleefully crushed under the hobnailed boot.

I was in Valletta one day, and decided to drop in for a beer. I entered the nearest hostelry, which was a Band Club – bar, café etc. Taking my glass from the counter, I moved to a table, sipped my beer, and observed my surroundings. These band clubs are all over Malta – during the spring, at the height of the season of village feasts, the bands play an important role in the celebrations, and they are a big part of Malta's rich culture. I noticed the barman emerging with a big tray, loaded with bowls of something – free snacks, I figured – and distributed them to the drinkers. Although I was the solitary one at my table, he generously had no intention of denying me my little free treat. He placed the bowl I front of me, and I instinctively 'thanked him very much' "Your welcome, Sir," he said, "have a nice day" Well, my eyes nearly popped out of my head, and my stomach lurched when I discovered the contents of the offering. Staring me in the face was a little army of Ireland's slimy, plundering, arch enemies, and to think that this was a tasty treat that I was meant to swallow, savour and relish!

I was glad when another man – a Maltese – placed his glass of beer on my table and joined me, diverting my attention.

The little evil army was now surrounded – but they were in no danger of an attack from me – although I did cop my table-mate eyeing them with a somewhat longing affectionate look. Alternating his gaze from the bowl to me and back again, I knew a strike was imminent. Making friendly eye contact with me, he smiled, pointed to the tank brigade and asked: "You no like?" I forced a return smile. "Oh, no, not at all, feel free, I'm just thirsty to-day." He thanked me profusely and preceded to scoff them all with aid of a tooth pick, that evicted the occupants from their tanks, and impaled nakedly on the spike, landed them on to the extended platform of his saliva-dripping tongue. My poor old mother, when she was ever in a threatening situation always said a little prayer, and I swear it came back to me that instant: *'God between us and all harm.'*

I decided to make a quick getaway, because I could sense the symptoms of an onset of nausea, and anyway, even my bloody glass of beer had turned sour. So I bade farewell to my snail gourmet, leaving him with his empty shells and his belly-full of goo. I have since discovered that snails are one of the most cherished delicacies in Malta. They are on the shelves of all good fruit and vegetable shops – I can't get my head around how the predator and his prey can happily occupy the same shelf, but they do - and they are in great demand at up to three Euro per kilo. Despite my total abhorrence at even the sight of the slimy little monsters, I have to commend the Maltese farmers for their shrewd enterprise. Instead of crushing them under their boots, they harvest them and turn a pestering nuisance into a lucrative extra crop. Now that's definitely one up on the Irish!

***

I have always been a lover of fresh fruit. I can't resist the soft, sweet varieties: bananas, grapes, peaches, plums, kiwis and apricots. In my own little garden back home I grow apples, strawberries, gooseberries, black currents, rhubarb and tomatoes, and with a little help from my freezer, they never go out of season – what a wonderful invention those freezers are, managing to thwart nature's rhythms, and serve up the goodies all the year round.

When we were children, I can't recall fresh fruit being a feature of our table, or any of our neighbour's tables either. Perhaps in those days the health benefit of fruit wasn't known or appreciated, or maybe it was the scarcity of funds that forced housewives to stick to the bare essentials, and fruit being a luxury, was only purchased for special occasions. But we did have plenty of one particular fruit when it was in season, and that was rhubarb. My mother was an expert at growing it, and because she had a knack of forcing it up with an abundance of well rotted farmyard manure, she produced a constant supply of juicy, organic rhubarb, bigger and earlier than anyone else. Of course, it was so bitter, that you couldn't eat it raw, but we had it in stews, in pies, and in giant tarts, smothered with sugar, and bubbling over with mouth-watering goodness. I can still taste my mother's rhubarb tarts to this day, and whenever I do, it reminds me of all the miracles these genius mothers performed, with big families to feed, and little or nothing with which to do it.

Malta is an absolute treasure throve of all kinds of succulent fresh fruit. At almost every corner I find a lorry laden with masses of ev ery variety under the sun, and for anyone to neglect their five-a-day here, it is certainly their own fault, and I, for one, gorge myself on it, and throughout every day, I feel the health benefit of it.

I must mention another fruit that in late summer and autumn, flourishes all over Ireland – the 'Blackberry' - and back in the days of severe austerity and poverty, when we were almost eating grass, it was a God-send to families like ours. The little blackberries smothered the hedgerows with juicy sweetness, and growing wild and free, provided food and welcome funds for many hard-pressed families. We picked buckets of them every year, sold them to the fruit factory for jam, earning vital shillings, and keeping us out of harm's way during the long school holidays. One of my vivid memories is the sight of barrels of blackberries being taken to the factory for processing, congealed, decomposing, with a strong stench, and a layer of mould on top. It gave off such a gassy odour that if you didn't know, you would have said it was more suitable for making aviation fuel than jam. That probably explains why those swanky pots of jam on the supermarket shelves never tempted me, I know too much about the ingredients.

I didn't find any blackberries in Malta, but I did find a fruit that also grows wild, and having seen it gracing the shelves of many 'Fruit and Veg' shops, at prime prices, I was surprised to find it growing by the roadside, freely available to pick and enjoy. I'm referring to the 'Prickly Pear' a seedy, juicy fruit, that I have recently learned, has been part of the stable diet of Mediterranean countries for thousands of years. It is the fruit of the 'Cactus,' and I suppose that's why it only grows in hot climates, and why, until I set foot in Malta, I had never seen it before in my life.

I was out walking one day, and above St. Paul's Bay I was passing a fairly large area covered with cactuses laden with eye-catching, orange-red pears. Feeling a bit peckish, I decided to have a little feast. Sure why not? They were wild and free, and if they're so good for the Maltese, they can't be too bad for an Irishman either. I waded in to get the biggest and best of the crop, and having landed my first catch, cupped and cuddled it lovingly in my soft, under-worked hands. Suddenly I realised something serious was happening to me, and what I was flirting with, was not a little harmless fruit, but a lethal weapon capable of inflicting torture to unsuspecting fools like myself.

What I didn't know – I do now – was that on the skin of the pear, are millions of sharp spines or needles, so thin that they are invisible, but they enter your tissue, remain there for days, driving you stone mad with pain and suffering. I never liked getting a thorn in my hand, and whenever I did, I immediately summoned the sewing needle, and out it had to come. Imagine how I felt when, through a harmless little misadventure, I ended up with a million prickly pear needles lodged under the skin of both palms of my hands. I'll say no more – it only brings the pain back – but in future I'll banish all memories of Malta's 'Prickly Pears,' and stick with my little humble and harmless Irish blackberry.

****

Cool and Trendy

I have just emerged from the darkness of the Internet café to the sun-soaked brightness of Tourist Street in down-town Bugibba. The clear blue sky and the absence of even a whiff of wind tells me it's going to be one of those gorgeous hot Malta days, with at least eight hours of bright sunshine, and floods of tourists milling around half naked, with broad smiles on their faces.

I find it amazing the effect weather has on Malta's visitors, especially the British. I know the main reason they're here is to escape the hideous winter climate back home, but they forget that it's the middle of January, and it's still winter here too. I readily admit that I forsake Ireland for Malta every winter for the very same reason, but I'm well satisfied with the package of weather I get here, and thanks to the 'Times' excellent weather forecasting, I know what's coming for five days ahead, and can plan accordingly. But for some unknown reason, that little bit of logic seems to escape those thousands of sun-seekers, who expect a clear blue sky every day, an extra layer of tanning on their backsides, and if one little cloud decides to have a pee, they act like drowned rats, scamper indoors with long grumpy faces that says: 'keep away from me…I'm having a bad day.'

Just like at home, Malta in winter serves up a variety of weather. Being a small, exposed island, it gets its fair share of wind, rain, and even thunderstorms, but mysteriously, it can change in a couple of hours from balmy sunshine to lashing rain, or from a windy, wet morning to a hot sunny afternoon. That's the difference between the climate here and the one we escaped from, and another important factor is the temperatures. Here it hardly ever drops lower than fifteen degrees, and in the middle of January, when it's minus three back home, and icicles hanging out of people's noses, how could anyone possibly complain about the winter weather in Malta?

I had no intention of travelling anywhere to-day, but looking across at the busy bus terminus, and the multitude of scantly-clad tourists heading off to various places, a little question pops out of my brain: 'Why don't you join them, Paddy, on this beautiful day, and revisit some old haunt, enjoy the ride, and leave the rest to your old friend: 'Fate?' Why not?' I answer, and precede to implement this impulsive prompt of my weird and unpredictable brain. It's funny, you know, this happens to me a lot, and for some reason that I can never fathom, it always works out well – I can't ever remember acting on an impulsive brain signal like that, and ending up regretting it.

I've just had another encounter with the bus-ticket machine, and having watched it spit out a day-ticket to my Maltese travel-mate ahead of me, for one price, and then to find that mine cost almost double what he paid, I'm again a bit peeved as I board one of those long bendy buses that

London banished from its wide thoroughfares, and Malta embraced with open arms to ply the narrow roads and congested streets of this little island. It hardly makes sense, but who am I to complain as I sit back in luxurious comfort, heading for two of my favourite resorts: St. Julian's and Sliema. It's no more than a stone's throw from here to my first port of call, but it's still too bloody far to walk, and, come to think of it, the bus fare I just paid, if calculated by the mile, would be a rip-off. I'll just have to stop this ranting – it's not enhancing my head or my heart – anyway, we're almost there already.

St. Julian's is almost unrecognisable from the little sheltered fishing village it once was – it is now one of Malta's busiest and most popular resorts. Most of it is new or upgraded, but one little spot, the real heart of the village, hasn't changed for centuries, and I hope it never will. Having just alighted from my big bendy bus on the corner overlooking St Julian's Bay, I can tell you, the picture-postcard scene in front of me is just captivating, with its quaint atmosphere and old world charm. I'm gazing down into the basin of the little cosy harbour, an eyeful of idyllic beauty. The little bay is awash with colour and activity. Anchored and weaving gently, are a little flotilla of traditional 'Luzzu' fishing boats, that always seems to be painted a more vivid red, blue and yellow here, than anywhere else around the island. Tucked away in the far corner, under the road level is the little ancient boat repair workshop, busy as ever, serving the fishermen, as it has done for many decades.

Around the perimeter, at water level, are a myriad of restaurants and cafes, booming with business, their sprightly staff like busy bees, darting in and out, serving the hundreds of diners sitting around open-air tables, flanked by the crystal blue water, under a cloudless sky, and soaking up the soothing rays of the smiling, hot sun. It's a paradise, and if it happens that heaven is better than this, I, for one, will be pleasantly surprised.

Of course, much of the development of St. Julian's is modern, trendy and upmarket. The new hot spot is Portomaso, and now that I've strolled up here, I can assure you that it is posh and exclusive. Dominating everything in the square is the giant 'Portamaso Tower,' a massive blue and terracotta office block, Malta's only skyscraper, and a landmark that is visible over a wide area. The world famous Hilton Hotel, with its extensive Conference Centre attached, occupies a prime location, and alongside is the private, state of the art marina, full of luxury yachts, indicating the presence of many well-heeled millionaires. No less exclusive, is the complex of fashionable apartments, chic, stylish and expensive, no doubt, owned and occupied by millionaires, because this is not an area for ordinary 'Joe Soap's,' - the whole idea is to attract the mega-rich, and I get the feeling that they have succeeded spectacularly.

I leave the grandeur of Portamaso and meander up town to a central maze of narrow streets full of cafes, bars and disco clubs. This is Paceville, the nightlife capital of Malta. This is the village that never sleeps, where the youth from all over the island congregate every night, especially at weekends, party and dance to loud music 'till the small hours, greatly antagonising the settled community with their exuberant shenanigans, and causing headaches for the police, who struggle valiantly to maintain peace and order.

I suppose it's a symptom of modern life in the trendy world we live in, and like all other western countries, Malta too has to deal with those three scourges: drink, drugs and prostitution, and Paceville is the hub of where it all happens. It's not yet as serious in Malta as in some other countries, but it is growing, and it is fast becoming an explosive package, that will inevitably blow up into a much more dangerous scenario: violence, criminality and even death. I hope it won't - Malta doesn't deserve to be blighted in this way. I have a hunch though, that with their wisdom and excellent record of law enforcement, the authorities will control it, and keep their little island the unspoiled gem that it always was.

Now on to Sliema, a little town that I always love to visit, and every year I come, I see it thrive and prosper with new innovations and improvements. The journey from St. Julian's to Sliema is a good mile to walk, but it never costs me a thought. The Tower Road that connects the two resorts winds around the scenic expanse of Spinola Bay, in a charming tree-lined promenade, lined with numerous cafes, bars and restaurants. It's a dream to stroll along at your leisure, and is always crowded with walkers, joggers and lots of snap-happy tourists.

Sliema stands on a headland enjoying two waterfronts, one flanking the Mediterranean, and the other looking across Marsamxett Harbour into the eyes of Valletta. This is where all the harbour cruise operators have their little jetties, and every day, all along the Strand Road, the persistent salespeople work the crowds, frantically courting business, and through their tenacity and sales skills, manages to fill the many cruisers with tourists of every nationality, take them to every nook and cranny of the Grand Harbour, returning them safe, highly impressed and delighted.

Apart from the harbour activity, Sliema is all about shopping. Up to a couple of years ago, the main shopping area was in the centre of the town between the two waterfronts, where many big international stores boomed, and were complimented by local independent shops, restaurants and boutiques. It was, and is still, a buzzing area of the town, pedestrianized and embellished to a high standard. But now, the development of Tigne Point has transformed shopping, not only for Sliema, but for the whole of Malta. This is located at one end of the town on an area jutting out into the harbour, and it is just massive. It comprises Hotels, apartments, entertainment, and a three-tier shopping mall, as good as you'll find anywhere in the world. The mall, in particular, is spectacular with at least one hundred of the world's top brand names located here - all the Maltese shop-oholics need now is loads of money. I must say that I'm hugely impressed with these wonderful new facilities, and I really hope it can flourish and prove successful, because this is a most courageous leap forward by the developers, and the government that backed them. All I can say is: well done and good luck!

While I'm here in Sliema, there's one other little place I want to visit. I discovered it a few years ago, and being just beside the bridge that links Strand Road with Manoel Island, it won't take me long to get there. I've arrived, and I must say 'The Duck's Village' looks as quaint and charming as the first day I spotted it. A little rocky enclosure, fenced off from the road with netting wire fencing, but with open access to the harbour, its population consists of hundreds of various fowl species: ducks, drakes, hens of all shapes and colours, guinea fowl, pigeons, and even multicoloured rabbits. They all live happily together in a little exclusive community, scratching around or swimming by day, and sleeping in little ornate coops by night. It is financed by voluntary donations, plus help from the local council, and since its creation about twenty years ago, has delighted children young and old, and thousands of tourists that were just lucky to find it.

Before I say goodbye to my little feathery friends, I must tell you about one day a few years ago I dropped in, and happened to have a video camera with me. I was filming away to my heart's content when I heard some commotion below me. A big monster of a 'Scoby Drake' had mounted a little timid duck, and was 'playing a blinder' in a frenzied sexual encounter. I felt mortified for the poor little duck – it was a complete miss-match – but who am I to judge? The little female had a look of ecstasy in her eyes, and of course, her big overweight jockey was thrilled with his ride. I still have that tape – it has generated many an Irish belly-laugh since- and it has copper-fastened my fascination with 'The Duck's Village' of Sleima.

****

Green Acres

'You can take the man out of the bog, but you can't take the bog out of the man.'
This old Irish saying could aptly apply to most of us Paddy's, including myself. I'm back to the old 'Sod' again, and because farmland is so synonymous with Ireland, it is ingrained in all of us, and no matter where we go in the world, we take a bit of it with us. I suppose that explains why I love to roam out into the rugged farmland of Malta, meander along narrow roads between dry stone walls, watch the old farmers lovingly tend to their vegetable crops, and feel a nostalgic contentment. For me it's a journey back in time, back to an era that I knew so well, the Ireland of my childhood, now just a distant memory, but still alive and well in Malta.

In their own way, the Maltese farmers work wonders with the meagre resources God gave them, and I'm always impressed with the enterprise and efficiency they apply to produce such quality and quantities of top class food for their families and their millions of guests. Having been used to the scale and intensity of Irish farming, my early forays through the land of Malta had me convinced that agriculture didn't exist here. I saw no farm animals, no machinery of any account, no big loads of produce on the roads, I just closed my mind and concluded that everything they ate, bar fruit and vegetables, came from beyond their shores. How bloody wrong can you be?

I now know that there are 16,000 cows and cattle, 70,000 pigs, 12,000 sheep, and 1.2 million poultry in Malta, and just because they weren't all grazing together in the little fields, I foolishly believed they didn't exist. But of course, like Ireland, the population of full-time farmers in Malta has slipped down in recent years. Farming a land-bank of around 12,000 hectares, keeps about 13,000 working full-time, but another 18,000 part-timers enjoy the best of both worlds – farming and working in the service industry. The core of real farmers that spend every day toiling in the heat of their fields are mostly elderly, and the thought of changing from their labour of love would never cross their minds. What happens when they pass on is another matter. The trend is towards part-time farming, and I suspect in years to come, when all these old diehards are gone, the whole industry will be highly mechanised, and run by part-timers.

I was strolling one lovely sunny afternoon out beyond Xemxija, through a maze of little vegetable farms, and I was in my element, soaking up the old rustic atmosphere, and the peace and solitude all around me. A little field of lovely cabbage prompted me to linger and admire the perfection of it. Not an inch was wasted, the rows were straight as gun barrels, and the crop was divided into various stages of growth. It was like steps of stairs, and clearly designed to mature in stages, and spread out the harvesting. I was impressed, and when I spotted the elderly man, in among the cabbages, hand-spreading fertiliser from his bucket, I chanced crossing the little wall to have a chat. Although he seemed a bit surprised at the intrusion, his bright eyes and broad toothless smile conveyed a genuine friendliness.

“Beautiful cabbage,” I ventured.

He just smiled.

“You sell to the hotels?”

Another smile.

The penny dropped. He hadn’t a word of English. I gave him my hand which he shook vigorously and smiled warmly. We parted, and I discovered later that when he was a boy, English wasn’t compulsory in the schools of Malta. Thank God, that has changed now, and all the younger generations of Maltese speak the language perfectly. English or not, I have to give my old farmer friend ‘top of the class’ for one subject: growing prize cabbages.

****

Ramble On

A recent article in the 'Times' caught my attention and confirmed a view that I have held since the first day I landed here: that the Maltese Islands are a rambler's joy, and I often wish I had the time and physical fitness to explore it. I learned from the article that the 'Ramblers Association of Malta' do wonderful work in promoting and conducting organised walks throughout the islands, and even grade them to suit the mobility levels of its members.

I wish I had known about this ten years ago when there was much less of me in it, and I could have avoided the extra layers of me, that have since padded my hulk and left me flabby, lazy and breathless. Maybe it's not too late yet. I see that their winter programme, just announced, includes over twenty different rambles, and although I know that some of the trails would be too demanding for a puffing snail like me, I might manage the lowest grade: *'for the occasional rambler who prefers leisurely stretches at a slower pace,'* – yes, I might try that one.

I love their blurb, designed to attract new members: *'This is the ideal time for wilderness rambling when the Maltese archipelago presents a floral paradise as the valleys, hillsides and country lanes burst into a riot of wild flowers in the shape of yellow capesorrel (qarsu), the sweet scented narcis and swathes of red clover.*' How could anyone with a shred of appreciation for natural beauty resist that – I'll definitely have a go, and you'd never know, I might be able to discard some of this excess body baggage out around the idyllic landscapes of Rabat or Dingli. I already have visions of a new slim more athletic me – why not? – stranger things have happened!

In the meantime, I've just stepped off the bus at one of the many villages that are sprinkled around the northern part of Malta, and the one that, after a less than inspiring first impression, I now always look forward to visiting. When I first discovered Mellieha many years ago, I was far from enchanted. Perched on a hilltop, it seemed a hard slog for a softy like me, climbing and descending its winding, narrow streets, coming to terms with its haphazard layout, and I wondered what possessed those ancient planners to site it there. But having survived its undulating terrain, I have come to love this little village, and return year after year for its beguiling beauty.

Mellieha has everything. Centuries of intriguing history, a panorama of breath-taking scenery, and a complex of underground caves and caverns. On a high plateau, overlooking the village is the parish church, a wonderfully impressive structure, and another example of the fine architecture of Maltese churches. Where, I often wonder, did all the money come from, back in the hungry nineteenth century, to build those massive basilicas in every little village? The mind boggles! I don't know the answer, but one thing I do know, they are masterpieces, everyone of them, and I delight in visiting them all.

But sure, any old village would have one church – Mellieha has two, one on top of the other! It's true – I better explain. When St. Paul was on the island in 60 AD, recovering from being shipwrecked offshore, it seems he was accompanied by his friend, St. Luke, the Evangelist. There was no big swanky basilica that time in Mellieha, but tucked away, and carved into the solid rock was a tiny chapel, which St. Luke, being handy with the brushes, decided to adorn. His painting of the Blessed Virgin, on the rock face, behind the alter, though a bit faded, is still there to-day. Although the big parish church stands almost directly overhead, the little cave church is still in constant use, and when I attend Mass there, I always get a special sense of spiritualism, unique to that little sanctuary.

Deep in the heart of this little village are a maze of rock-cut shelters where the people took refuge during the Second World War to escape Hitler's cruel aerial bombardment. I took a trip down one day, and I have to tell you, the experience shook me. Isn't it amazing how a people under siege, with their lives and their children's lives at stake, will use their wits and their courage to withstand deadly attacks of terror and firepower, and endure the most appalling hardship to survive.

Down in those cramped shelters I saw living quarters, hewn from the rock with bare hands and primitive tools, I saw little makeshift hospital wards where babies were born and the sick attended to, and I saw the system of regulation and order that was applied to preserve privacy and dignity, a must in such crowded underground living. I can only imagine what it must have been like down there for weeks on end. My one hour trip was more than long enough, and when I emerged from the dark to the welcome brightness of the day, I was still overwhelmed with bewilderment, but also with respect and admiration for the resilience and durability of those brave survivors, most of whom are now, sadly, gone underground again.

Now, for all you lovers of hot sand and cool water, sun-worshippers who love to lie out on a hot beach with little more cover than a smile and a pair of sun glasses, I'm sorry to be the conveyor of disappointing news – you won't find much of it in Malta. Yes, there are sandy beaches, but they are few and far between, and for the most part the shoreline is rugged and rocky, ideal for good swimmers, but really not for beginners. One exception is Mellieha Bay, where you'll find a beautiful white sandy beach, and stretching for half a kilometre, it is easily the longest in Malta.

From where I'm standing now, on the highest vantage point of Mellieha, the beach forms part of the glorious panorama of landscape and seascape that stretches for miles on all sides of me. Sloping gently into the blue Mediterranean, its lovely fine sand can compare with any in the world. It's just a pity there's not more Mellieha Bay's around Malta, because although it is almost deserted to-day, it can be crazily congested in summer, and to enjoy a bit of sunbathing and swimming during the busy season, you would need to be an early bird.

Of course, the scarcity of sandy beaches here is in itself a motivation for the development of many other water sports: sailing, speed-boating, and particularly diving. Diving is really big here, and is the attraction for many overseas visitors. Some tourists devote their whole holiday to the sport, and because Malta's underwater world is so magical, diving schools and centres have sprung up all over, and have become big business. There are at least twenty-five safe diving sites, including shipwrecks, and the centres cater for all levels of divers – excluding my level, of course, being one of those species that can only swim like a hammer.

So, you see, it's back to the old saying again: *'it's an ill wind that don't favour someone,'* The divers don't miss the sandy beaches; they are happy exploring their own little underworld, and at the same time bringing in valuable extra revenue, and helping to boost the economy of Malta.

***

There are days when I love to ramble and roam through the wide open spaces and fresh clean air of Malta's countryside, and there are days when I yearn for the cosmopolitan atmosphere and bustling vibrancy of Valletta, but one little environment where I am always totally at ease, is the old city of Mdina. I'm not sure why an old medieval town should hold such a grip on my affections, but it does, and I can only conclude that it's the rare contemplative feelings it evokes, a kind of escapism, a getting away from it all to a different world of ancient history, to a haven of peace and solitude.

For those of you that haven't yet experienced the magic and mystique of Mdina, and perhaps are unaware of its history, I'll briefly give you a short synopsis. The capital and stronghold of the Arabs, who conquered Malta in 870, and stayed there for two centuries, it was inherited by the Knights of St. John, who restored it to its current form. Located strategically on the highest point of the island, it is fortified on all sides by massive walls, and surrounded by fertile agricultural countryside. After 'The Great Siege' of 1565, the Knights built their new city of Valletta, moved bags and baggage, and left Mdina to rest peacefully in redundancy and retirement, and it has been known ever since as 'The Silent City.'

But of course, it refused to die, and even to-day, this magnificent citadel, though relieved of its ancestral power and influence, is still capturing the imagination of multitudes each year, who come here from all over the globe, and will not leave without being captivated by its mystery and intrigue. I happen to be one of them, and when I enter through the splendid main gate – built in 1724 – and walk those narrow paved streets, I always get a strange eerie sensation, as if I'm trespassing on hollowed ground, accompanied by the ghosts of centuries past, and knowing that this once important seat of power, influence, and activity, is now slumbering in quiet solitude and peaceful tranquillity.

The little streets cut through tall elegant buildings, are so narrow that a handshake from opposite footpaths is easily attainable, the old municipal buildings are embellished in rich Maltese tradition, and the facades and entrances of the many old mansions, some draped in flowery foliage, are oozing elegance and charm. Statues and sculptures adorn street corners, the old administrative offices are now important museums, and from a vantage point high up on the ramparts, I'm mesmerised by the heavenly panoramic view of almost the whole Island of Malta.

Dominating the main square is undoubtedly the jewel of this ancient city: 'The Cathedral of St. Paul.' Built in 1693, rising majestically above the whole city, dwarfing all around it, this church is regarded – by experts on the subject – as the finest example of baroque architecture in all of Malta, and it is also crammed with a magnificent collection of important works of art. The nearby 'Cathedral Museum' is also a must for visitors, because it is to-day considered as one of the most important museums on the island.

To-day, Mdina is no longer silent. Restaurants, cafes and shops enjoy booming business, and life for the four hundred inhabitants is, I expect, similar to that of any other little community. But it still has some magnetic force that draws *me* back time after time, filling me with awe and admiration for those leaders, diplomats and revered figures of traditional Maltese society, that once walked these medieval streets, and now only their ghosts remain to evoke mystique and memories, and imbue us visitors with wonder and intrigue.

***

I don't know about you, but exploring the underground was never something that appealed to me or got me excited. I am well aware that multitudes of people simply love it, and would be happy to spend hours down there. But no, I'm definitely not one of them. The way I look at it is: one of these days I'll be forced down, and lump it or like it, I'll have to stay, so why should I be in any hurry to head down there prematurely.

I'm making this point because within a stone's throw of Mdina is the charming town of Rabat – as old as 'The Silent City' itself, and with almost as much to explore underground as over it. Now, I'll be honest and admit that I was never down in the famous early Christian Catacombs, or the maze of tunnels that lie beneath the streets - a complex underground world that stretches to over a square mile. Those catacombs were ancient cemeteries from the fourth century onwards, and I'm reliably told that down there is a fascinating collection of burial chambers and tombs, where ritual funerals took place, and thousands of people are buried. Of course, evidence of all this is there to be seen to-day, as two sets of catacombs are open to the public, and I have seen with my own eyes a constant stream of tourists enthusiastically heading down – I never had the slightest urge to join them.

In contrast, I never leave Rabat without calling to St. Paul's Church in Parish Square and visiting the famous grotto, an ancient little cave chapel set deep in the rocks underneath the parish church. This is truly intriguing, because it is where St. Paul took refuge during his three-month stay on the island in 60 AD, after being shipwrecked, and it appears as if nothing of his little abode has been touched or changed in almost two thousand years.

The town itself is quaint and beautiful. I love the traditional character of the narrow streets, and the lines of old-style houses with their ornate Maltese enclosed balconies. But Rabat is also a busy town of 13,000 residents, a commercial hub for much of central Malta. On the outskirts is Buskett Gardens, a small wooded area of shade and tranquillity throughout the year. Back in the era of the Knights it was a hunting reserve for the Grand Masters, and their palatial palace – erected in the 16th century – is still used to-day as the official summer residence of the President of Malta.

So, you'll agree, there is much to see and enjoy in the historic town of Rabat – including many little old pubs – and because they are side by side, I always fill a whole beautiful day with the fascinating delights of Mdina and Rabat.

****

Malta's Little Sister

It's a bright Wednesday morning and I'm rolling along in my little self-drive Peugeot towards the big ferryboat at Cirkewwa, eagerly looking forward to a pleasant day-trip to Malta's little sister island, Gozo. I have religiously done this every one of the ten years since my relationship with the Maltese Islands began, and I have to say that its therapeutic sustenance has never waned. In fact, a few years ago, I became so besotted with this little island that I extended my vacation in Malta, and spent an extra two weeks in idyllic Xlendi Bay, from where I criss-crossed the rustic landscape every day; so pleasant and fulfilling that I could have stayed forever.

Gozo is the second largest island of the Maltese archipelago, and compared to the pace of its big sister, it's really a little haven where time stands still. There are other notable differences too. It's so small – 14 KM long by 7 KM wide – so green – little family farms, rich and fertile, producing an abundance of milk, eggs, potatoes, tomatoes, melons, oranges and figs. No wonder it is referred to as the market garden of Malta. Of course, fishing is important too, and the little fleet of colourful boats bring in a tasty and varied supply for the 30,000 residents and their guests.

For me, there is another aspect of Gozo that is different from Malta. Nowhere will you find people so genuinely friendly and charming, and no matter where I roam, visiting all the quaint little villages, I'm received with a warmth and a welcome that I find unique and wonderful. Possibly it's because Gozo is an island of great religious piety, with every little village featuring a beautiful church that would adorn any large city, and it could also be because the big arrogant, modern world hasn't been embraced here, kept at arm's length, while they preserve and protect their cherished traditional values.

I've just squeezed my little car in among the hundreds of other vehicles on the car deck of the 'Ta Pinu' – one of the two ferryboats run by the Gozo Channel Company – and I'm climbing the stairs to the passenger decks. These are fine modern ships, with every facility for the comfort of travellers, and being a lovely calm day, I'm expecting a smooth passage that will take me to the exquisite little harbour of Mgarr in less than half an hour. I can relax in the lounge, browse the book shop, or enjoy a good coffee and snack in the cafeteria; I do neither, and proceed to the top open deck, where I join dozens of like-minded others, to inhale the breezy freshness, watch the rich blue sea scurrying away from our disturbance, and to get an eyeful of the picturesque, lonely island of Comino, which we pass close-by on our way.

Comino lies halfway between Malta and Gozo and covers just one square mile. Although practically uninhabited except for one farmer family, one hotel, and one tiny chapel, it is still a big attraction for large numbers of tourists in summer. They come to explore the barren, sun-baked rock, but their main attraction is the famous 'Blue Lagoon.' This is a tiny cove of incredible turquoise waters, rippling over a bed of fine white sand, and it is brilliant for swimming or diving. I've spent a day in this heavenly bay, and I have to tell you, I have never seen water so colourful or beautiful. I have no idea where the turquoise comes from, but it's a unique phenomenon, and judging by the numbers of pleasure craft ferrying swimmers, snorkelers, divers and day-trippers to this idyllic spot, it is becoming a huge tourist attraction. It's at a times like these that I regret not being a swimmer – I can only imagine the pleasure of soaking the body in that 'holy water' – but sure, never mind, I content myself with a good leg-wash, and an extra bit of tan, as I watch the water-hens all around me frolicking in ecstasy.

We have disembarked, and I'm now exiting the stylish new port terminal of Mgarr. This used to be a 'stone age' port facility, but two years ago the government upgraded it - at a cost of many millions - and now it is 'state of the art,' and a gift for the thousands who use it every day. Unfortunately, the same can't be said for the terminal at the Malta end – it is still 'stone age' – but it too, is earmarked for development and hopefully, will soon be as swanky and modern as the one in Gozo. This ferry service is important to Malta and Gozo. Last year the two ships between them made 20,000 crossings, carried 1.1 million vehicles, and ferried 4.1 million passengers. There is much speculation about developing a direct link between the two islands – an underwater tunnel or some other connection – but at present the huge cost of such a project is the big deterrent. I can see it happening in the future, whether I'll be around to test it out is anyone's guess; I'd like to think so, but sadly and frustratingly, it's not in my hands. Please God I will.

As I drive out of the port and up through this little harbour village of Mgarr, I'm captivated by its picture-postcard natural setting. The greatest artist that ever lived couldn't do justice to this beauty – the lines of colourful little boats anchored in the dock, the quaint, honey-coloured houses, the tapestry of tiny green fields above and beyond, and the blue waters of the Mediterranean caressing the shore. All I can say is: 'Tis great to be alive!

I'm on the main road to the capital of the island, Victoria, and I must say, compared to what this road was like when I first came here, it is now a modern highway. You can't beat EU money, and Malta is not shy in accepting it. Fair play to them, they have used it wisely for the benefit of their citizens and their guests.

As I enter Victoria, I again get the feeling that nothing much ever changes here. A few modern buildings and shops on the outskirts, but as I go into the centre, it is the centuries-old buildings that give it the charm and character that I love so well. The square is a real gem – beautiful old buildings, quaint pubs, cafes and restaurants, and a myriad of market stalls selling everything under the sun. The atmosphere and buzz here is mighty, and enlivened even further by a group of middle-aged buskers playing and singing rousing tunes to the delight of the tourists that come here from all over the world.

Those visitors, having consumed the delightful ambience of the square, then climb the energy-sapping hill to the medieval Citadel, with its fortifications, cathedral, museums, and magnificent views. This is the centrepiece, not only of Victoria, but of all Gozo. Towering high above since the fourteenth century, it can be seen from every corner of the island, and when I walk around its massive bastions, I can see all of this idyllic island, its lush green landscape, and the blue Mediterranean enveloping it.

The seventeenth-century, baroque cathedral, perched on top, is a big attraction for visitors. It was for me too, but alas, not anymore – the reason for which you will soon discover. Designed by Lorenzo Gafa, it is a work of art, and although I only had the pleasure of one visit, I was impressed by the interior, adorned with side alters, sculptures and paintings. A little story relating to this church fascinated me. The building was near completion, except for the most important feature of all Malta's churches: the dome. Sadly, they had run out of money. It was a most embarrassing predicament, but they pooled their wits and came up with an ingenious solution. They engaged a famous Italian artist who incredibly, painted a false dome inside, and looking up, you couldn't tell the difference. What a clever idea.

Not so clever is the practice of the present-day custodians to link entrance to the cathedral with entrance to the museum, and apply an admission charge for entry to both. I discovered this a few years ago when I was entering the cathedral, and had no time or inclination to visit the museum. I was abruptly stopped at the door and told to buy a five Euro ticket, as I had to pay and visit both to visit one. Of course, Paddy blew a fuse! Despite my protestations, there was no derogation, so I swivelled on my heels, headed back down the steps, and haven't troubled them since.

Now, I have a thing about churches; I can't resist the temptation to drop in – especially those beautiful basilicas in Malta – but I also have a thing about paying to go in; I point blank refuse, and I will argue my case with anyone. I'll put it this way – if the man that started all this religion 2,000 years ago were to return, what would he say? He would sack all those lightweights – that believe they are a law unto themselves – and he would reverse much of their misguided handiwork. That now, is my little rant for to-day, so, having decided once again not to bother climbing those punishing cathedral steps, I head out of town into the beautiful countryside to visit a church that over the years has inspired pilgrims from all over the globe – me included – and to further warm my heart, it is totally free of charge.

When I first came to 'Ta Pinu Sanctuary' ten years ago, I experienced a strange peace and tranquillity, a solace and solitude that I had often yearned for, but only found here. It is now my special church in all the world, and back home in my little homestead in Ireland, its image hangs prominently, and is admired by friends and neighbours who haven't had, like me, the privilege of experiencing its heavenly blessings.

Its history is intriguing and fascinating. It all began in 1883 when two local villagers Karmni Grima and Francesco Portelli heard a mystical voice calling from within the church as they walked by. They entered and prayed for Francesco's desperately ill mother, who miraculously recovered. From then on, the miracles multiplied. Now, thousands of pilgrims come and kneel before the ancient shrine of 'Our Lady,' plead for cures and favours, leave in peace and hope, knowing that they have already received a blessing, Attached to the church is another shrine, this one dedicated to the thousands of anguished pilgrims from near and far, who came with their afflictions, were cured, and returned with heartfelt gratitude to place on the shrine, pictures, mementoes, and their discarded aids; testament of the miracles performed by Our Lady of Ta Pinu.

Although Gozo is small, and easy to scoot from one corner to another, there are so many little beauty spots to revisit, that I can't linger too long in any one place, so, having had my little chat with 'Our Lady of Ta Pinu,' I head over to the coast and the exquisite little inlet, Dwejra Bay. This is a site of incredible natural beauty, the views are just spectacular, the sea is blue and inviting, and it's a walkers paradise. Every visitor to Gozo feels compelled to visit this unique attraction, especially to see the little 'Inlet Sea' and the Azure Window.

The 'Inlet Sea' is a tiny basin of sea water surrounded by high cliffs, where local boatmen take tourists on little trips out through the amazing rock tunnels into the open sea. The 'Azure Window' is now a world famous rock formation, a haven for divers, and the most photographed attraction in Gozo. I have hundreds of pictures of it on my SD cards, but still, each time I return, it stands up there in all its mysterious charm, cheekily posing in front of me.

On my way back from Dwejra, I pass through the quaint little village of San Lawrenz, where the world famous writer and novelist, Nicholas Monsarrat spent his final years. I suppose that for an icon of the waves, that gave the world 'The Cruel Sea,' it was no surprise that he chose this peaceful little hamlet, overlooking the blue Mediterranean, to end his days. Like myself, he loved the Maltese Islands, and his other great masterpiece, 'The Kappillan of Malta,' recalling the 'World War Two' heroism of the Maltese, was written in this little hideout.

Though sadly, the master is now gone, his simple dwelling is still here, and when I pause and ponder, I'm always imbued with awe, remembering the literary genius that once graced this spot, and seeing the view he enjoyed from his writing desk by the window, I'm not surprised by his decision to be buried at sea – for a legendary sea-lover, what could be more appropriate. Appropriate and fitting too, was the decision of the villagers to name one of their little streets 'Triq Nicholas Monsarrat,' a tribute to a world famous legend, and an appreciation of his affection for Malta, Gozo, and especially San Lawrenz.

I head back again to the 'cross-roads' city, manoeuvre my little Peugeot through the narrow streets of Victoria, on my way to another little love-nest of mine, Xlendi Bay. Halfway there, I make a brief stop at the village of Fontana. This ancient hamlet gives me real connection with the hearts and minds of the people of this tiny island. At both sides of a little hillside square, crystal clear water is flowing from the rocks into old stone baths, where in years gone by, the women came with their baskets of clothes, laboured through the week's washing, and probably had a chat and a good laugh too.

The old baths are still there, though they are now silent except for the music of the water, still flowing, but long made redundant by the advent of the washing machine. Not redundant though is the little square, which is once again a hive of activity. Three big shops selling genuine Maltese handcrafts are doing booming business, particularly the one specialising in local handmade lace. This is an old Gozitan craft, highly prized for its quality. I've been in there and was captivated by the sheer skill and artistry of these ladies of lace. It's no surprise that every tourist coach visiting Gozo has this little village of Fontana as a stop on its itinerary.

On to Xlendi Bay, (pronounced 'Shlen-di') another little haven of idyllic charm. Beautifully placed at the gateway to a long picturesque valley, and hidden by two tall rocky promontories, it is a delight for swimming, diving, or just strolling around. During summer, the sheltered little dock is packed with a myriad of pleasure craft, but to-day, only the little boats of the local fishermen are here. In peak season too, the dozens of little bars, cafes, and restaurants are crowded, but to-day, only a handful of diners are eating, and many of the restaurants are closed for the winter. But I like it this way. The towering high rocks, the blue of the ocean, the little boat repair yard, and the scenic beauty of it all, can be viewed and appreciated much better in the absence of an overcrowded mass of tourists.

That's why I came here for two weeks in the winter of 2006, and enjoyed the comfort and quietness of 'St. Patrick's Hotel' – *why wouldn't I, with a name like that?* I can tell you, I savoured every minute of my fourteen days, strolling the hills and valleys, rambling through the old lanes and little fields, and absorbing the soothing peace and solitude of this world apart. From this homely base, I navigated my little car to every corner of the island, and when it was time for me to say goodbye, I felt blissfully revived, happy and refreshed, and rejoicing in the wonder of God's creation.

I pledged to return sometime for another taste of heaven, and after a lapse of six years, I suppose it's near time now to honour that pledge. And when I do, I hope this charming little retreat will once again inspire a little poem, like it did in 2006.

Xlendi Bay to see I came,
A passing glance, no more.
But welcome beamed from every hill
And smiled along your shore.

How could a lonely traveller I,
Resist this call sincere.
I'll come again before I die,
I said, perhaps next year.

And now I'm back to nestle in
Your tranquil loving breast.
My soul enriched and blessed within
Your heavenly peace and rest.

From my past experience of visiting Gozo, a one-day trip is never enough. You see and enjoy so much, but you have to go, and leave so much unseen. My fleeting visit to-day took me to just a few of my favourite haunts, and they certainly warmed my heart, but if I came again to-morrow, I could call on as many more, and be equally enchanted. Places like: Marsalforn Bay, the little fishing harbour with its fleet of colourful boats, waterfront restaurants, cafes, and its famous old saltpans, Ramla Bay, a unique beach, with its famous red sand, and the fabled Calypso's Cave, where, according to legend, Calypso kept Odysseus a 'prisoner of love' for seven years, Xaghra village, and the prehistoric temples of Ggantije, the oldest free-standing buildings in the world, a UNESCO World Heritage site, the charming hilltop villages of Nadur and Zebbug, Xewkija, with its narrow streets and magnificent church, and Gharb, with its folklore museum – a house with twenty-seven rooms, filled with Gozo's fascinating history.

I could list many more gems which I have discovered, enjoyed and long to revisit. God willing, I'll be back – that's for sure – and in the meantime, I'll savour the anticipation of returning, and perhaps writing more volumes to describe and eulogise this little paradise of Gozo. Today's brief glimpse of the island and its lovely people may engage *your* imagination, and perhaps sometime in the future, you may wish to see it for yourself. If you do, I can promise you an inspiring and rewarding experience.

****

Time to Go

I have now enjoyed three weeks here, and as my wish was to share the good news of these little islands through the medium of this book, I have resisted the gang, and their temptations to live it up. I'm not sure if I can hold out much longer. You see, Sunday is my birthday, and I have heard on the grapevine that plans are afoot. I can guess what they are, and I fear the consequences. So, in case this pen may become incapacitated, I will now bring this to a dignified conclusion.

I have given just a tiny taste and a bird's-eye view of Malta, my little haven of tranquillity. Its attraction for me is two-fold; the mystique and beauty of its history and landscape, and the simplicity and sincerity of its people. The pen does not adequately convey these characteristics; they must be experienced and enjoyed. There is something solid and re-assuring about the Maltese. Perhaps their strength is derived from centuries of defensive heroism against greedy predators, and their eventual glorious triumphs over pain and adversity. Whatever drives them, Malta is now a proud Independent Republic, with a healthy democracy, a prosperous economy, a distinctive language and culture, and a deep-rooted Christianity that inspires all their thoughts, words and deeds.

Some famous geologists have speculated that the Maltese Islands, being just a little 'rockscape' peeping above the waves of the Mediterranean, may be susceptible to an earthquake, or a future giant Tsunami, and could be submerged into oblivion in minutes. I can never see that happening. If courage, piety, honesty, and sincere generosity, are virtues recorded on high as bonus points, Malta will prevail into the distant future, in peace and prosperity, illuminating the Mediterranean as a beacon of light for the world. So now, as an Irishman, coming from that *'green and misty isle,'* I would like to finish with a tribute to *"My Gem in the Med,"* with my version of the world renown, old marching song:

It's a long way to Malta
It's a long way to go
It's a long way to Malta
To the sweetest place I know

Goodbye Piccadilly
Farewell Leicester Square
It's a long, long way to Malta
But my heart is there

****

The Crying Sea
Paddy Cummins

A **Maltese** fishing boat explodes in a raging inferno and sinks to the depths of the Mediterranean.
So begins six days and nights of unspeakable anguish for the crew; shock, horror and grief for the island of Malta.
Inspired by a true sea disaster …
A harrowing story of intense human drama.

"A superb read … A story that will remain with you forever."

Damien Tiernan. Author of: 'Souls Of The Sea'

Bridge Publishing

Also by
Paddy Cummins

At Home in Ireland

Spare Ride

Green Lodge

Shades of Life

Fields of Green

The Bombing of Campile

The Crying Sea

Time and Tide

Yoke the Pony

Bridge Publishing
The above books are available to purchase on
www.amazon.co.uk